A SURVEY OF THE EDUCATION OF GIFTED CHILDREN

By

ROBERT J. HAVIGHURST, EUGENE STIVERS

AND

ROBERT F. DeHAAN

The Committee on Human Development
The University of Chicago

THE UNIVERSITY OF CHICAGO PRESS

Supplementary Educational Monographs

PUBLISHED IN CONJUNCTION WITH *The School Review*
AND *The Elementary School Journal*

NUMBER 83 · NOVEMBER 1955

Library of Congress Catalog Card Number: 55-11415

THE UNIVERSITY OF CHICAGO PRESS, CHICAGO & LONDON
The University of Toronto Press, Toronto 5, Canada

PREFACE

There has been so much interest and activity concerning the education of gifted children in recent years that it is hard to keep abreast of the march of events and even harder to get a perspective on the variety of things that are happening. This survey is an effort to do both these things.

The text consists of a statement of criteria for a good program of education for gifted children, with illustrations of how the five criteria are met in practice. There is also an attempt to trace relations between types of programs for gifted children and types of communities or clienteles which support these programs.

The longest part of the survey is a set of summaries of the programs of about forty-five schools, school systems, and projects for serving gifted children. These are intended to give the reader a grasp of the major details of what is actually being done in the schools that are doing the most for talented youth.

Finally, there is a list of bibliographies and a selective bibliography of recent publications concerning gifted children.

The detailed work of searching the literature and of summarizing the reports of school programs has been ably and industriously done by Eugene Stivers.

For financial assistance in the conduct of this survey we wish to thank the Fund for the Advancement of Education.

ROBERT J. HAVIGHURST

TABLE OF CONTENTS

Page

I. CRITERIA FOR A GOOD PROGRAM OF EDUCATION
OF GIFTED CHILDREN   1

II. VARIETY OF TALENT   4

III. SYSTEMATIC DISCOVERY OF CHILDREN WITH
A WIDE VARIETY OF TALENTS   6

IV. MOTIVATION OF GIFTED CHILDREN 13

V. USE OF COMMUNITY RESOURCES 18

VI. METHODS IN THE SCHOOLS 20

VII. SUMMARIES OF PROGRAMS FOR GIFTED BOYS AND GIRLS   33

Birmingham Public Schools, Alabama 34
North Phoenix High School, Arizona 35
West Phoenix High School, Arizona 36
Berkeley Public Schools, California 37
Los Angeles City Elementary Schools,
  California 39
Los Angeles City Secondary Schools,
  California 40
San Diego City Schools, California 41
Evanston Township High School, Illinois 43
New Trier Township High School,
  Winnetka, Illinois 45
Francis W. Parker School, Chicago 46
Quincy Public Schools, Quincy, Illinois 47
University of Chicago Laboratory School,
  Chicago 48
Indianapolis Public Elementary Schools,
  Indiana 50
Thomas Carr Howe High School, Indianapolis,
  Indiana 52
Cedar Rapids Public Schools, Iowa 53
Atchison Public Schools, Kansas 54
Children's Summer Studio, Lawrence, Kansas 55
University of Kansas, Department of Art
  Education Program for Children, Lawrence,
  Kansas 56
Baltimore Public Schools, Maryland 57

B. B. Russel School, Brockton, Massachusetts 59
Worcester Art Museum, Massachusetts 60
Worcester Girls Club, Massachusetts 60
John Burroughs Intermediate School, Detroit,
  Michigan 61
Edwin Denby High School, Detroit, Michigan 63
University City Public Schools, Missouri 64
Fieldston School, New York City 66
Hunter College Elementary School, New York City 67
Sewanhaka High School, Floral Park, New York 68
New York City Schools
  Division of Junior High Schools 70
  Division of High Schools 72
  Public School No. 241 73
  Bronx High School of Science 74
  Brooklyn Technical High School 76
  Forest Hills High School 78
  High School of Music and Art 80
  Stuyvesant High School 81
Cleveland Public Schools, Ohio 83
Ohio State University School, Columbus 84
Dayton Boys Choir, Ohio 86
Malvern Elementary School, Shaker Heights, Ohio 86
Portland Public Schools, Oregon 87
Allentown Elementary Schools, Pennsylvania 90
George School, Bucks County, Pennsylvania 91
Pittsburgh Public Schools, Pennsylvania 92
Colfax Elementary School, Pittsburgh,
  Pennsylvania 94
Dallas Public Library, Texas 96
The Program for Early Admission to College 97
The School and College Study of Admission with
  Advanced Standing 98
The School and College Study of General Education 99
The Horace Mann-Lincoln Institute of School
  Experimentation 100
The Science Talent Search and National
  Science Fair 101

BIBLIOGRAPHY 103

CHAPTER I

CRITERIA FOR A GOOD PROGRAM OF
EDUCATION OF GIFTED CHILDREN

This survey was undertaken in order to get an up-to-date view of developments in the rapidly changing field of education for gifted children. A list of school systems, individual schools, institutions, and organizations was prepared. Each of them was supposed to have a current program of unusual merit for the education and development of gifted children. The list was obtained mainly from the Yearbook of the American Association for Gifted Children, edited by Paul Witty and published in 1950. A few other programs were added because they had been noted in recent publications.

In addition to this list of programs of special merit or interest, a further list of schools was included--schools with a very good reputation for general excellence but without any special program for gifted children. Without exception, these were favored schools--favored either because they were private schools with unusually good facilities or because they were public schools in favored communities, drawing their pupils from families which are predominantly upper middle class and spending about twice as much per pupil as the average in their respective states. Several of these schools had taken part in the Eight-Year Study of the Relation of School and College sponsored by the Progressive Education Association in 1932-40. The reason for including these favored schools in this survey was that there seemed to be some basis for a belief that such schools do as well for gifted children without a special program for such children as does the more nearly average community school system with a special program for a selected group of gifted children. The report will show some evidence that this is true.

We wrote to all the schools and other institutions on our list, sending them a questionnaire and asking them for information about

their program. Almost all of them answered. We believe that all those
with any strong claim to consideration did answer.

There probably are some schools with very good special programs
for gifted children which we have overlooked. We doubt that there are
as many as a dozen, however, which were overlooked but nevertheless
have as good quality as the ones described.

There certainly are many good and favored schools which are just
as good as the small number we have selected to represent that group.
Readers who know American schools will recognize that the small group
we chose to study in the category are simply illustrative of the much
larger number of such schools.

*   *   *

It is said that in a certain city in California there is a program
for the development of tennis talent. This community has been producing
excellent tennis players for several decades--players who regularly
appear in the top ten of California and often make the national selections. This community proceeds as follows:

There are tennis courts in public parks and school grounds, freely
available. School children are encouraged to play tennis. Those who
show promise are identified early and given lessons by coaches employed
by the city recreation department. A series of tournaments for players
of various ages brings the winners to public attention. The best
players are discovered and given expert coaching, free of charge.

The schools are a searching and proving ground for tennis talent.
The community rewards tennis talent with public approval, free coaching, and scholarships when young tennis players get ready for college.

This community, year after year, turns out a high quality of
tennis players, in numbers much larger than those provided by other
larger cities which do not have a systematic program for discovery
and development of talent.

If such a program were applied to all forms of socially desirable
talent, we would have the ideal situation.

*   *   *

From observing the actual situation in a number of communities,
we have drawn up the following set of criteria or characteristics of
a good program for gifted children. This is the structure of ideas

within which the problem of educating gifted children will be analyzed.

A good program for gifted children.--

Aims to develop a variety of talents;
Has a systematic program for the discovery of a wide variety
  of talents;
Seeks to motivate gifted children to make use of and to develop
  their talent;
Makes use of a variety of community resources in the development
  of talent, in addition to the schools;
Uses effective methods of teaching, curriculum materials, and
  administrative procedures in the schools.

CHAPTER II

VARIETY OF TALENT

A successful program of education for gifted children aims at
the development of a variety of talents. It is one purpose of a
democratic educational system to assist in the development of the
constructive potentialities of its students, whatever these potentialities may be.

A meaningful definition of the gifted would then not be a nar-
row one but might include every child who, in his age group, is
superior in some ability which may make him an outstanding contribu-
tor to the welfare of, and quality of living in, society.

Programs operating on this basis seek to develop such a variety
of gifts and talents as:

    a) General intellectual ability (ability to think abstractly
       and do other kinds of relational thinking) and its various
       components, such as reasoning, verbal skill, mathematical
       skill, and spatial imagination

    b) Ability in such useful areas as science, mechanics, social
       leadership, and human relations

    c) Talent in creative arts, such as graphic art, music, creative
       writing, and dramatics

From what we know about the nature of talent, we suppose that
there is relatively little connection between the various kinds of
talent. While it is true that there is a tendency for gifted
people to be talented in more than one area, there certainly are a
great many people with talent in only one area and no more than
average ability in most other areas.

While talents are varied and talented children are often no
more than mediocre in their untalented aspects, there are relatively
few schools or communities that attempt to provide stimulation and
assistance in the development of a wide variety of talent. The
Portland public school program has perhaps the widest range. In
this program children are identified and encouraged if they have

high levels of ability in graphic art, musical ability, mechanical
arts, dramatics, creative writing, rhythms, and social leadership,
as well as in general intelligence.

The New York City schools also offer programs to develop a
variety of talents. Special classes for the gifted in elementary,
junior high, and high schools include most of the areas of the curriculum, while several specialized high schools offer work in art,
music, science, mathematics, and technology. In addition, the size
of the schools and the facilities at their disposal permit advanced
course offerings in special fields and co-curricular activities that
develop a variety of gifts and talents.

There is also a small number of first-rate public and private
schools that have an extraordinarily varied set of offerings,
although they may make no special effort to select and encourage
the talented children. These schools tend to attract children of
generally high levels of ability. They are usually in economically
favored communities which can afford to offer a program of wide
scope and high quality generally. Such schools are usually found
in the economically favored suburbs of cities, while a number of
private schools and university laboratory schools also come in this
category. Examples among the schools in this survey are: George
School (Pennsylvania), Fieldston (New York City), New Trier (near
Chicago), University of Chicago Laboratory School, Ohio State
University School, Francis Parker (Chicago), Malvern (Shaker
Heights, Cleveland), Colfax (Pittsburgh), University City (St.
Louis).

CHAPTER III

SYSTEMATIC DISCOVERY OF CHILDREN WITH A
WIDE VARIETY OF TALENTS

A successful educational program for gifted children is based upon a systematic procedure for the discovery of children with a variety of talents.

Potential talent is not easily recognized unless the child is placed in situations which bring out his talents. Such situations need to be systematically provided. It is also recognized that systematic testing as well as observation should be used for the discovery of talent.

There is a threefold importance in looking for a variety of talent in children. First, such discovery points out to teachers that there are other bases besides intelligence for talent in children. Second, it calls attention to more children than a single-talent criterion does. Third, it encourages the teacher to use a variety of avenues of approach to children, whereas a single measure of giftedness narrows her approach.

The actual methods used to identify talented children tend to combine the two logical extremes of simple nomination by teachers and a battery of objective tests. Neither extreme has been found to be desirable, although both are sometimes used for reasons of convenience or habit. If teachers' nominations are to be used, the teacher must have objective criteria with which to judge the children's ability, as well as established rules of observation. She must also be given some kind of supervisory help, so that she can talk over and learn from the nominations that she is making.

The strength of using teachers' nominations is that they are efficient, they involve the teacher psychologically in a program for gifted children, and they require her to use a high level of ability. The disadvantages of using teacher judgments is that they are unstandardized from teacher to teacher and are of varying reliability.

The value of objective tests lies in the fact that they provide data which are independent of teachers' judgments and are standardized from classroom to classroom. The difficulties in using objective tests consist primarily in the fact that they are cumbersome and inefficient from the school's point of view. Tests of many of the talents are still to be developed, and at present we must rely on rather crude instruments. And, finally, there is almost inevitably a lag between the time that the teacher gives the test and the time that the results are reported to her.

There is substantial improvement being made, both in the method of teacher nominations and in testing procedures. For example, an attempt is under way in Quincy, Illinois, to provide teachers with more objectified observational instruments. A handbook is being developed for teachers which deals with a number of distinct kinds of talent, along with behavioral characteristics of these talents. Teachers are asked to observe these characteristics in children and record systematically the names of the children who display them. Suggestions for objective tests to be used in the classroom are also given in the handbook.

Efforts are being made to develop objective tests in the areas of the fine arts and leadership. The work in this area tends to be limited to university research agencies and a very few school projects.

Most school projects operate this part of their program in a restricted and unimaginative way. Tests tend to lie unused in cumulative folders. Children who do not behave or achieve up to the level indicated by their test results are sometimes discredited by unimaginative teachers. Rarely is a list of names of gifted children drawn up and put "on the conscience" of a given school staff or community agency. Two programs have rather concentrated on the identification of a variety of talents. These are Portland, Oregon, and Quincy, Illinois. The examples will be taken mainly from these projects.

Methods of Screening for a Variety of Talent
Which Go beyond Teacher Nomination

Varieties of nonintellectual talent which can be discovered are the following: social leadership, artistic ability--dramatic, mechanical, musical--creative writing, and rhythmic ability. General

intelligence itself is also made up of a variety of relatively independent abilities, such as verbal, mathematical, and spatial. At
the present time, we are able pretty well to discover the "primary
mental abilities" by using objective intelligence tests.

The solution to the problem of objective testing for a variety
of talent is, first, to obtain a product of the child in a specific
talent-area and, second, to evaluate the quality of the product.
The evaluation should be done by experts in each specific field, or
at least the standards of judgment and examples thereof should be
provided by experts. Let us take each of these areas, one at a
time, and show how they might be tested and give illustrations of
how they have been tested.

a) Social leadership.--This can best be done through teachers'
ratings and through sociometric devices. An instrument used on the
Quincy project to get teachers' ratings is the Behavior Description
Chart.[1] This is an instrument by which a teacher is able to report
systematically her observations on children.

A second method for testing for social leadership used in the
Quincy Youth Development project is the "Guess-Who Test".[1] This is
a sociometric test administered to the children. They are given a
list of all their classmates and are asked to put the names of the
children by the items that describe them. This gives a peer evaluation of the behavior of children and yields leadership scores.

In the Portland public schools, Portland, Oregon, an attempt
has been made to develop a complex identification instrument for
leadership. Three nominating sheets were used in this instrument.
The first was a sheet which was to be filled in by teachers and group
leaders. These adults were asked to list the names of children who
appeared to them to have leadership qualities. The second nominating
sheet was given to the entire class of children from whom leadership
identification material was to be obtained. The children were asked
to name children who would be the best leaders in a particular thing
that the class had to do. The children also were asked to write why

---

[1]Described in Paul H. Bowman and Others, Studying Children and Training Counselors in a Community Program. Supplementary Educational
Monographs, No. 78. Chicago: University of Chicago Press, 1953.

they thought the person they named was a leader. The third nominating
sheet, also a sociometric instrument, listed five different characteristics of children, such as "those who are nice to everyone, help
others, and are admired by other pupils," "those who have a lot of
interesting things to do and games to play," "those who can take charge
of a group," "those who stand up for other people's rights," "those
who are the best in sports." The children were asked to name children
who showed these characteristics.

b) The test of art abilities.--The Quincy Youth Development Commission developed the Four Drawing Test for use with fourth- and
sixth-grade children in 1952. The children were asked first to make
a Drawing of a Man, using the standard Draw-a-Man instructions by
Goodenough.[2] Second, they were asked to draw a picture of their
classroom as it was seen from the doorway. The third assignment was
to make a landscape. The final assignment was to be a free choice of
anything that they wished to draw. These drawings were then rated by
a number of people in the community who were interested and had ability
and experience in art. The children were ranked in the order of their
ability.

This rating procedure required the participation of a large number
of judges and was fairly time-consuming, although in a repetition the
amount of time spent could be cut down drastically.

The Portland public schools used primarily the same procedure in
screening for young artists, though their assignments were somewhat
more stimulating than the ones in the Quincy project. They asked the
children to draw such things as a picture of a Battle Royal; a picture
of something that they did at home; a picture of the Prettiest Spot on
Earth; a picture of a Good Time; and then another free choice. The
drawings were done at the fifth-, sixth-, seventh-, and eighth-grade
levels. The first screening was done by the classroom teacher who
selected the top 20 per cent. This was spot-checked throughout the
whole city. The second screening was done by three committees of
teachers who were set up in different areas of the city. Teachers
on these committees were chosen on the basis of their knowledge of

---

[2] Described in Florence Goodenough, <u>Measuring Intelligence by Means of
Drawings</u>. Yonkers-on-Hudson, New York: World Book Co., 1926.

art. A final screening was done by a committee of art specialists.

The Quincy project is using a somewhat different test in 1955.
The attempt is that they are tested not only on a global ability
but also on smaller specific assignments. One assignment is to
draw a number of specific things that might be found in a storeroom
or secondhand store, such as a lamp, a table, a cup and saucer, etc.
In another assignment they are asked to draw the expressions on the
faces of people in various situations. In a third assignment they
are to compare various objects within given spaces. They are also
asked to draw pictures of a "stick-man" in various poses. The
global assignments are to draw pictures of a blind man walking down
the street with a girl, a boy running toward a house, a still life,
and the inside of the classroom.

c) <u>Dramatic ability</u>.--Portland has made considerable progress
with screening for dramatic ability. A committee of teachers and a
dramatics consultant make the rounds to the schools and give the
dramatics test. The children are asked to pantomime, to read a
script from a play, and to act out certain incidents. The children
are then rated by the consultant and by the people on the committee.

d) <u>Tests for mechanical aptitudes</u>.--In the Portland system
three sources of identification data are used. First, the industrial
arts teacher must select a child who constructs the best project and
who generally works in the mechanical areas quite proficiently.
Second, the children are given a chance to rate their peers on the
products that they produce in the shop. Third, the California test
of mechanical aptitude is given to these youngsters. Only the boys
are tested, since the girls do not take shop as part of their program.

e) <u>Testing for musical abilities</u>.--The Portland public schools
give the children a questionnaire on their musical activities and on
the musical instrument that they play. In the second part of the
test a record of various kinds of music is played, and the children
have to mark whether the music is a walk, a march, a gallop, or a
slide. In the third part of the test the children have to decide
whether the music is happy, sad, sleepy, or mysterious. In the
fourth part they are to say whether the record played was like a cow,
a bird, a bear, a bumblebee, a rabbit, an elephant, a frog, or a
horse. Finally, the children are asked to decide whether a given

tone is the same pitch or different from another one that was played.

In Quincy the Gretch-Tillson test for musical aptitude is given. This test is an adaptation of the Seashore test. It is given in the elementary school, the parents of the children who score high are notified, and the children are given a chance to take instrumental lessons and to play in the band.

f) Creative writing.--Quincy began to test for creative writing in the winter of 1952 by asking the children to write paragraphs on some of the following subjects: the most exciting event that had happened to them; a letter to grandmother; an editorial on some aspect of school life.

In Portland a somewhat more specific creative-writing test was given. The children were given barren sentences which they had to make more descriptive and picturesque. They were also asked to write stories from lead sentences and to write stories about objects in the room. These assignments were stimulating to both teacher and children.

In Quincy it is planned to develop a test which has a number of sections to it. One section will be on developing picturesque sentences, a second on describing their friends (adult and peers), another on telling stories.

g) Tests of rhythmic ability.--In Portland a committee developed criteria for judging rhythmic ability. They developed a group test for primary children. The committee then went around to schools to test children for this ability. In the test the teacher would beat on a drum to determine which children could keep time to this rhythm. The children were also asked to act out what was suggested to them in musical records. For example, a record was played of a snowplow pushing snow. The children then had to act like snowplows. In another item the children had to pantomime and act out an animal scene. From this the teachers, as a committee, then judged the rhyth- mic ability of the children.

h) Creativity.--The quality of creativity is poorly understood, and there are no established methods of measuring it. Yet people persist in searching for it and trying to define and measure it, because they feel that this quality does exist and that it is the most precious of talents when combined with a specific talent of one

kind or another. At present there are some psychologists[3] attempting
to learn more about creativity, but no school has a plan for identifying creative children.

The procedures for discovering talent reported here are in the
developmental stage. For some time they can be expected to change
quite rapidly until acceptable procedures in each area are worked out.

---

[3] J. P. Guilford, "Creativity," _American Psychologist_, Vol. V
(September, 1950).
L. L. Thurstone, "Creative Talent," _Invitational Conference on
Testing Problems, October 28, 1950_, pp. 55-69, Princeton, New
Jersey: Educational Testing Service, 1951.
M. I. Stein, "Creativity and Culture," _Journal of Psychology_,
XXXVI, (1953), 311-22.

CHAPTER IV

MOTIVATION OF GIFTED CHILDREN

Having discovered the talented children, the next step is to
help them develop the determination to make something of their potential talents. This is a major problem which is seldom recognized
as such by the people who have been bemused by the myth that "talent
will out." This myth has been supported and spread in the past by
a few striking examples of geniuses whose talents flowered in poor
environments, plus the pervading belief that inheritance was more
important than nurture in human talent. Only within the present
century have we learned enough about the nature of human abilities
to recognize the fact that most of the potential talent of preceding
centuries has not been developed and that at present at least half
of our best human material is not developed to anywhere near its
capacity.

Lack of motivation is the main reason why half of the ablest
quarter of our youth do not go to college; lack of motivation surely
robs us of at least half of the high-level talent that we might otherwise have in other areas, such as art and music.

It is in keeping with American social ideals to state the basic
proposition that all talented children should be given full opportunity to develop their talents. The only exceptions we might make
would be those that bar one sex or the other from certain activity
areas--such as women from military careers. With this small qualifi-
cation, we can state it as an accepted proposition that all potentially
talented children should be encouraged and given the opportunity to
develop their talents.

When the environment is not favorable, the talent seldom develops.
But the environment has to be favorable in certain special ways.
Human talent differs from the potential for high-level performance
found in race horses and milk cows and wheat and fruit trees, in that

13

the quality of motivation must be added to favorable environmental qualities for its fruition.

Children must want to develop their talents if they are to succeed in making the most of themselves. Lack of motivation may result from:

Ignorance of one's potential ability
Emotional disturbance
Lack of good work habits
Parents' indifference or hostility to the particular talents
    which their children possess
The community's indifference or hostility to the talents which
    certain children possess
The community's attitude that certain talents are not appropriate
    for certain groups of children--for girls, for boys, for
    Negroes, etc.
Lack of opportunity to display talents and be rewarded

Types of Motivation

In order to move with any degree of assurance on a program of motivation, we need a basic knowledge of the types of motivation and their sources. This knowledge is incomplete, but we know enough to make a good beginning. The motivation of a boy or girl to work hard at the development of a talent may have three forms:

a) <u>Achievement motivation</u>.--This is a tendency to do one's best at anything or almost anything one tries. It is a generally high aspiration level. Apparently, this is developed quite early as a part of the basic personality; but studies are now under way to find out how to modify it.[1]

b) <u>Intrinsic motivation</u>.--This is a deep desire to carry on a certain kind of activity for the joy it gives. The person would work at development of a talent without any thought of reward or approval from outside himself. This is found in people who like to paint, to make music, to dance, and to read, or to tinker with a motorcycle.

c) <u>Social motivation</u>.--This is a desire to develop a certain talent because of the prestige it will bring, because it will please

---

[1]See David McClelland and Others, <u>The Achievement Motive</u>. New York: Appleton-Century-Crofts, 1953.

one's parents, or because it will bring rewards of other kinds from
the social environment.

Methods of Initiating and Increasing Motivation

The possible ways of increasing motivation are the following:

Giving information about a child's abilities.--A good many
children possess unusual potential abilities without ever becoming
aware of them. This is true particularly of certain intellectual
qualities, such as spatial imagery, which are not cultivated or discovered in the usual school curriculum. But it may also be true of
artistic talent or dramatic or musical talent in families which do
not naturally encourage their children in these areas. Consequently,
the mere giving of information about a child's abilities to him and
to his parents may stimulate him to seek training or otherwise to get
experience that will begin to activate one of the motivational forces.

This procedure is followed in a number of places, including
Cedar Rapids, Cleveland, Portland, and Quincy. In the Quincy program
a graph is made for each talented child, showing his relative standing
on measures of various aspects of talent. A counselor shows this
graph to the child's parents and discusses it with them. A similar
procedure is being tried out, experimentally, with some of the
children. In certain cases the disclosure to a child that he has an
I.Q. of 130, for example, whereas his school achievement has been only
average, has resulted in much greater effort at school work.

Wherever the talented children are separated out in special groups,
it may be presumed that this procedure has a motivating effect on
parents and children to some extent. But a personal interview with a
guidance specialist may have greater motivating effect, since this
gives an opportunity to discuss the specific types of talent shown
by a particular child and to consider definite steps which parents
might take on behalf of their child.

Guidance.--On the basis of knowledge about a child's special
abilities he can be guided into classes, clubs, and other experiences
which will help him to develop these abilities. Guidance is the
device most generally and most consciously used by schools to motivate
their abler pupils. It is stressed in the reports from Brooklyn
Technical High School, New Trier, Forest Hills, Bronx High School of

Science, Sewanhaka (New York), Cleveland, T. C. Howe High School of
Indianapolis, Baltimore, Cedar Rapids, West Phoenix, North Phoenix,
George School, and Francis Parker (Chicago).

Counseling.--Also, where the achievement motivation of a child
is low because of faulty character and work habits, there is a possibility for counseling and psychotherapy with the child and with
his parents. It is probable that as we learn more about achievement
motivation, we may find that it is a personality characteristic which
can be affected by counseling. If so, pupils with potential talent
but low achievement motivation will become a target group for
counseling.

Program-building.--When children already have incipient interests, the opportunity to try out these interests will prove a
motivating experience for them. Thus a school with an orchestra,
science club, drama group, and leaders' club has gone some distance
toward increasing the motivation of children with talents in these
areas. Many schools have such programs, but New Trier High School
is a particularly good example. A varied program in a particular
field may promote motivation, as demonstrated by the science department of Forest Hills High School.

Providing models.--The school can bring talented children into
close contact with attractive and talented adults, both on the school
staff and in the community. Here the example set by an attractive
young chemist, engineer, artist, musician, or writer will serve to
increase the motivation of teen-agers who have some potential ability
in these areas. This is practiced by Evanston, and T. C. Howe high
schools, North and West Phoenix, New York High School of Music and
Art, Pittsburgh, Bronx High School of Science, and Brooklyn Technical
High School.

Giving rewards.--Social motivation can be maximized in a school
by setting up a system of rewards for those who make a good achievement in a wide range of areas. There may be prizes, publicity for
especially good work, honor rolls, and honor societies. There may
be assemblies in which the outstanding performers are honored.

A widespread form of social motivation is the contest, used
especially in the area of science. The Science Talent Search is a

powerful motivating influence and is reported as an important aspect
of their program by Forest Hills, Bronx High School of Science, Stuyvesant, Evanston, and North and West Phoenix. Science fairs are
reported from several places, including Pittsburgh, Indianapolis, Los
Angeles, San Diego, Berkeley, Bronx High School of Science, Stuyvesant,
and Forest Hills.

Scholarship awards are a special type of award which has motivating value as well as financial value. Pittsburgh makes special use of
this method through the Allegheny County Joint Committee on Scholarship Aid.

CHAPTER V

USE OF COMMUNITY RESOURCES

The nonschool resources in the community can be used on behalf of gifted children in two different ways.

Skill-training Groups

Community institutions may set up programs more or less independent of the schools. For instance, the Dayton Boys' Choir, the Dallas Public Library, the Worcester Girls' Club, the University of Kansas Department of Art Education, and most of the art museums of the country offer opportunities to talented children without any particular relation to the schools, though the schools often aid in selecting children and encouraging them to take advantage of these opportunities.

The Dayton Boys' Choir, sponsored by the Rotary Club, consists of 90 boys, aged nine to eighteen. The Dallas Public Library has two creative writing groups of 20 each, one for high-school pupils and one for elementary-school children. The Worcester Art Museum has classes in the afternoons and Saturday mornings for 1,250 pupils. The Department of Education at the University of Kansas offers special art instruction to 75 children of the city of Lawrence. The YWCA in Quincy offers Saturday morning classes in painting and in dramatics. The Los Angeles City Library holds a library class twice a month for gifted children.

Where science is stressed heavily, as at Forest Hills in New York, students may be placed in laboratories as assistants, to learn more and to get closer association with scientists. In Detroit certain business and industrial companies offer supervised experience for talented students from Denby High School.

School-initiated Projects

The schools may take the initiative to exploit community resources for the sake of gifted children. Most commonly this is done

18

through field trips and visits by children to places and people of
interest in the community. For example, Public School No. 241 of
New York uses the Brooklyn Botanical Garden and the Brooklyn Museum.
The Francis Parker school in Chicago sends pupils on as many as
thirty field trips to mills, farms, churches, courts, housing projects, stores, concerts, and sand dunes. Colfax Elementary School
in Pittsburgh makes extensive use of field trips, and children visit
the Carnegie Central Library every three weeks for books and research.
San Diego schools send groups of students to the Mount Palomar and
Griffiths observatories. New York City junior high schools make
studies of local community problems and encourage the abler pupils
to take part in community programs for civic improvement.

Often the schools will invite distinguished citizens to come
and meet and talk with pupils. This is done mainly in the high
schools, such as T. C. Howe in Indianapolis, North and West Phoenix,
Pittsburgh, Evanston, Bronx High School of Science, and Brooklyn
Tech.

CHAPTER VI

METHODS IN THE SCHOOLS

There are three general procedures whereby a school can stimulate gifted children and help them to develop their abilities. Enrichment is primarily a teaching procedure, while special grouping and acceleration are administrative devices. Any two of these can be combined, and all three can be combined, but it will be useful to consider them separately.

Enrichment

Enrichment consists in giving the gifted child an opportunity to go deeper or to range more widely than the average child in his intellectual, social, and artistic experience. Enrichment alone, not accompanied by acceleration or special grouping, keeps the talented child in his own age group and with children of various levels of ability.

The nature of the unusually capable student is such that enrichment in its most productive form consists not of adding more of the same kind of content and activity to the program but of providing experiences in greater variety and at a more advanced level. Such a program may be characterized by (1) emphasis upon the creative or the experimental; (2) emphasis on the skills of investigation and learning; (3) independent work, stressing initiative and originality; (4) high standards of accomplishment; (5) co-operative planning and activity that provide opportunity for leadership training and experience in social adjustment; (6) individual attention given by teacher to student; (7) firsthand experiences; (8) flexibility of organization and procedure; (9) extensive reading, and (10) concern with community responsibility.

Some enrichment programs consist of assignments, projects, or units of study of sufficient scope and complexity to allow the most gifted children to use and develop their talents, while the average child works with the same assignments but does not go so far with

20

them. Another form of enrichment is supplementary project-work performed by abler pupils, in addition to the regular work as performed
by average pupils.

Enrichment may also be provided on a lateral, extensive basis,
encouraging the abler children to broaden their experience by working
in areas not explored by the average student. The gifted child may do
work in the arts, in music, creative writing, industrial arts, and
foreign language while in elementary school. This can be done through
special-interest groups set up by the schools and other community
agencies for children of a range of ages.

A disadvantage of purely lateral enrichment is that a given child
may not be interested in lateral extensions of his experience. He may
be primarily interested in deepening a single area, such as science or
arts. The kind of deepening enrichment which he demands is difficult
to provide without special grouping of children. In short, some gifted
children can profit from a lateral or broadening type of enrichment,
while others will not be motivated by such offerings and will demand
deepening of their present interests.

Hunter College Elementary School has a "club period" in which
children of similar interests get together for special group activities which are shared with the other children in school assemblies
and classroom projects. Portland makes considerable use of lateral
enrichment at the elementary-school level. In the Malvern School at
Shaker Heights (Cleveland) the abler pupils do extra work, such as
heading committees for group projects, performing experiments for
the class, making speeches in class on behalf of the Red Cross and
community fund drives. Cedar Rapids and Pittsburgh have bulletins
of suggestions to teachers, aimed to help them provide within an
ordinary class a broader and more advanced experience for the gifted
child. Sewanhaka High School offers assignments of greater depth,
supplementary work, and more varied experiences to its gifted students
in the regular classroom.

A practical disadvantage of enrichment in the regular classroom
is that it often places an intolerable burden on already overloaded
classroom teachers. Enrichment in the classroom is not easy for a
teacher to manage.

Advantages of enrichment practices lie in the fact that they
are cheap, easy for school principals to administer, and do not
unduly single out the talented child for special consideration.

Special Grouping

The abler children may be placed in special groups for all or
part of the school day. The purpose of special grouping is usually
to provide for enrichment of children's experiences, in both depth
and breadth, and to permit the children to stimulate one another.
Another purpose, that of acceleration, is also sometimes served by
special grouping. The usual plan of special grouping is to pick
out the ablest children on intellectual bases and put them together
for a special enriched program. This may be pushed to the extent of
placing gifted children in a special school, as at Hunter College
Elementary School; or it may consist of bringing the gifted children
from several schools together in a single special group, as at
Allentown, Pennsylvania; Brockton, Massachusetts; Birmingham; and
Indianapolis. The Cleveland "Major Work Groups" represent this
type of grouping in a program which has been going successfully
for about twenty years. More commonly, it consists of grouping
pupils by intellectual ability into two, three, or four groups, depending on the numbers of children of a given age. This is often
done at the beginning of junior high school, as in the John
Burroughs Intermediate School of Detroit.

A common form of special grouping is to place talented youth
in special groups for a part of the school week--one or two
periods a week or as much as one or two periods a day. Colfax
Elementary School in Pittsburgh has a program of Workshops for
Gifted Children during a part of the day. University City (St.
Louis) has an ingenious plan of "enrichment classes" that meet once
or twice a week under a special teacher. These groups average about
ten in size and carry on special projects which are often shared
with the school through an assembly program or a presentation to a
particular grade group. Thus these classes are something like
clubs and special-interest groups, such as orchestra, band, and
speech classes. Sewanhaka High School offers a seminar for gifted
Seniors. Each student member selects and plans an activity
related to one or more of his regular subjects, and in the weekly

meetings students and faculty discuss the study projects.

Los Angeles elementary schools have a Special Work Program for Rapid Learners, which involves approximately 100 pupils gathered from 24 schools. They meet one morning a week in groups of 12-15 with their Special Work Program teacher.

Special grouping does not start in Berkeley, California, until the seventh grade, when pupils are placed in ability groups on the basis of intelligence tests, achievement tests, and teachers' judgments. However, Berkeley provides a number of special music and art groups for talented elementary-school children.

An important form of special grouping is the specialized school, illustrated by the New York City high schools, among which are two for students with special ability in science and mathematics, one for those with mechanical ability, and one for students with talent in music and art. In addition, eight academic high schools in New York have separate "schools" for the gifted within their regular school organizations, where the abler pupils are segregated in practically all areas except health education, study hall, and lunch. Further, there are special classes in 42 New York City high schools for students of superior attainment in particular subjects.

Area programs.--Special grouping makes it relatively simple to provide for special interests of children. Where this is the aim, the children may be placed in ordinary classes with a heterogeneous group most of the time and then be selected for special classes in the areas of their particular interests; or they may be placed in special classes or schools for the entire program.

Science.--Pupils with scientific talent are frequently put into "honors classes" or special classes. For example, the Forest Hills High School (New York) offers a three-year program of honors work in biology, physics, chemistry, and mathematics to a special group of about 40 students from each ninth grade. North Phoenix High School offers a special program for about 65 of its ablest science students.

Foreign language.--Study of foreign language is sometimes started in the elementary school, with gifted children separated into a special group, as in Allentown. At the high-school level the George School has a foreign-language division in which those with special language interests may concentrate on combinations

of Latin, French, German, and Spanish. Within the language division
there are three classes, sectioned by ability.

Mathematics.--A number of high schools offer a four-year mathematics program to students with special ability and interest. For
instance, New Trier (Chicago), West Phoenix, George School, Stuyvesant, and Bronx High School of Science (New York) provide the
equivalent of the ordinary first-year college work in mathematics,
and students who take these courses may enter courses in calculus
as soon as they reach college.

Arts.--Special work in the arts is more widely available than
is such work in most areas. This may take the form of a special
school, such as the High School of Music and Art in New York City,
or art instruction offered by out-of-school agencies, such as the
Children's Summer Studio operated by the Municipal Recreation
Department of Lawrence, Kansas; the afternoon and Saturday morning
classes of the Worcester Art Museum; and the Saturday and summer
classes conducted by the Carnegie Institute for the talented
students of the Pittsburgh schools.

Music.--Another area of special work is music, usually offered
as choral and instrumental music to students with special interest
and ability. This area may be covered by a school program, as in
Berkeley, or as a community project, such as the Dayton Boys' Choir
and the music department of the Worcester Girls' Club.

English arts and social studies.--Several high schools have
special classes in these areas, including New Trier, Forest Hills,
Denby, George School, and Sewanhaka. The Dallas Public Library
offers special classes in creative writing.

Conditions Which Favor Special Grouping and
Conditions Which Favor Enrichment

Enrichment may be provided without special grouping or with
it. The argument in favor of special grouping is that it facili-
tates enrichment. But there is a considerable body of opinion
that is opposed to special grouping and in favor of classroom enrichment.

"Enrichment of the program in the regular classroom seems to
be the best solution to the problem of meeting the needs of gifted
children in most school systems," says the bulletin of the Austin

(Texas) public schools, published in 1954 under the title <u>Curriculum</u> <u>Enrichment for Gifted Children in Regular Classes</u>.

But in the larger communities and in cities where the number of children per classroom averages about 40 and there are no special teachers for music, art, or other special fields, the tendency is to resort to some form of special grouping as a means of enriching the experience of the abler children.

This practice is recommended with great caution by the Educational Policies Commission, which says:[1]

Special classes for the gifted may be used in schools with large enough enrolments to make them administratively feasible. However, the dangers and disadvantages of the plan should never be ignored. In some circumstances, strong objection to the plan by school staff, student body, or community may in itself be sufficient reason for avoiding its use. Evidence on the relative advantages and disadvantages of grouping gifted students in separate classes for some of their school work is still inconclusive. Well-controlled long-term experimentation to determine the values and limitations of such grouping is greatly needed.

Since the Educational Policies Commission made this statement (in 1950) there has been considerable growth in the use of special grouping.

A tentative generalization can be made concerning the conditions under which special grouping is likely to be adopted. When communities are divided, as shown in Table 1, on the basis of size and of socio-economic status, it is the large, average-type community that is most likely to use special grouping, while the medium-sized, favored community and the small, average-type community are least likely to use special grouping.

A "favored" community as the term will be used here is an upper-middle-class suburb of a large city. Such communities are fairly homogeneous as to socio-economic status and send 80-90 per cent of their high-school graduates to college. They may spend twice as much money per pupil on their schools as does the average community, and their schools have relatively small classes, are extremely well equipped, and have relatively well-trained teachers. Perhaps it is significant that such communities seldom claim to have a program for gifted children. For instance, Winnetka (Chicago) and Bronxville

---

[1] <u>Education of the Gifted</u>. Washington, D. C.: Educational Policies Commission, 1950.

TABLE 1

Type of Community in Relation to Use
of Special Grouping

Is this community likely to use special grouping for gifted pupils?

Size	Socio-economic Type of Community	
	Average	Favored
Large	Yes	(Nonexistent)
Medium	Uncertain	No
Small	No	No

(New York) do not make such claims. The Malvern School in Shaker
Heights (a suburb of Cleveland) belongs in this category of schools.
It relies on enrichment in the regular classroom, as do the elemen-
tary schools of Winnetka and Bronxville and similar communities.

The average I.Q. of children in such communities is a great deal
higher than in the average community, and there is a tendency,
encouraged by the parents in this type of community, to attempt to
treat all children as though they were at least headed for college,
if not actually gifted.

Closely related to the favored community schools are the "good"
private schools in our survey. They draw their pupils mainly from
upper-middle-class homes, and the average I.Q. in such schools is
likely to be 120 or above. These schools also tend to rely upon
enrichment without special grouping. This is true of Fieldston,
Francis Parker, University of Chicago, and Ohio State University
schools. While there are usually a number of small special groups
in such schools, these are interest groups, clubs, and activity
groups rather than talent groups.

In general, it seems safe to say that the favored communities
and the private schools serving upper-middle and upper-class
families tend to avoid special grouping as far as possible and to
count on small classes, well-trained teachers, well-equipped

schools, and special-interest projects and activities to supply enrichment for both gifted and average children.

The large, average-type American city is most likely to use
special grouping for gifted children. The larger cities have tens
of thousands of school children and thousands of teachers and thus
are in a position to make good use of specialization. Special
groups of many kinds can be set up efficiently and economically with
specialist teachers.

The larger cities generally have large classes--sometimes with
40 or more children in the average elementary-school classroom--
which makes it difficult for teachers to work out enrichment procedures for individual pupils. In these circumstances it is natural
to set up special classes of smaller size for gifted children and
for any other groups which deserve special treatment. Special
treatment for special groups is more likely to be acceptable to the
public in a large city than in a smaller city, because people in a
large city expect variety and specialization in city services.

Furthermore, the people of a large city tend to be anonymous to
one another and therefore are not very much interested in what class
the neighbor's child is in or whether the neighbor's child gets into
a school group which is taught differently from the group their own
child is in. Special classes in the schools are not so highly
"visible" to parents in a large city as in a smaller one. Those
whose children are not in the special classes may be ignorant of the
existence of a special program which in a smaller city could be
construed by some people as showing favoritism toward some families
and their children.

New York City has gone further than any other in providing special
groups for gifted children. Other cities which were studied in the
survey and fit this generalization are Birmingham, Los Angeles, Indianapolis, Baltimore, Detroit, Cleveland, and Pittsburgh.

Exceptions to this generalization are to be found in Portland
and San Diego, where the schools, after doing a careful job of identifying gifted children, keep them in the regular classroom and work out
methods of special treatment with limited special grouping. In this
respect these cities are more like the medium-sized average type of
city, where it is uncertain whether the program will lean toward

special grouping or toward enrichment in the regular classroom.
Allentown, Brockton, and Atchison use special grouping, but Cedar
Rapids and Quincy do not. Berkeley, Caifornia, uses ability grouping at the junior and senior high school levels. University City,
a suburb of St. Louis, is a favored community but uses a limited
type of special grouping which is more like a special-interest program than like a program for gifted children.

Special grouping is more likely to be found in high schools than
in elementary schools, for the obvious reason that students' programs
are differentiated according to their aims and interests in the high
school, thus providing a basis for further differentiation according
to ability.

Thus a number of favored communities have special grouping in
high school but not in elementary school. Examples are New Trier and
Evanston (both suburbs of Chicago), Sewanhaka (Long Island), and the
George School.

The small, average community generally does not use special
grouping, partly because the numbers of children are too small to
permit economical special grouping and partly because the small community is relatively cohesive and therefore tends to resist any grouping
of school children that promotes heterogeneity. There is not much to
be seen of education for gifted children in this type of community.
Probably anything that is done will have to rely upon club programs
led by talented adults in the community, together with county-wide
special classes for work in the arts, dramatics, etc.

The foregoing generalizations should be qualified by recognizing
that powerful or persuasive individual persons in the community can
create programs that do not fit the general pattern. The superintendent of schools may determine whether there is to be special grouping
or not, particularly in the medium-sized average community. A strong
principal may create a program in his own school which runs counter
to the trend in a city. A committee of citizens, especially in an
undecided medium-sized community, might successfully put its weight
on the side for or against special grouping.

Summary of Community Factors Affecting the Program

Thus we can see that the nature of the school program for gifted children depends in a fairly predictable fashion on the following factors:

1. Size, complexity, and wealth of the community, which affect:
    A. Expenditure per pupil
    B. Class size
    C. Possibilities for specialized assignments to teachers
    D. Possibilities for special schools and special classes within schools

2. Social structure and social values of the community, which determine:
    A. Whether people will tolerate a variety of school programs for various socio-economic and interest groups
    B. Whether special emphasis is put on programs for one or another group of children, e.g., slow learners, crippled children, intellectually gifted, artistic, musically inclined, athletic

3. Leadership in the community (lay or professional), which determines:
    A. Whether the community will lead or follow the procession in setting up a program for gifted children.
    B. What kind of program shall be adopted in communities where the other forces working for or against special grouping are fairly evenly balanced

Acceleration

Acceleration offers opportunity for a gifted pupil to move at a pace appropriate to his ability and maturity and to complete an educational program in less than the ordinary amount of time.

One form of acceleration is grade-skipping; another is steady progress through a particular series of grades in less than the usual time; and a third is early entrance to school or college.

Skipping is the promotion of pupils on the basis of past high-quality performance into classes or grades at a higher level than their age would ordinarily allow, then requiring the regular work of the new level.

Acceleration of this kind may consist of pushing a child rapidly through a barren curriculum which for him is little more than busy-work which he can do more quickly than other pupils. Although this may have the advantage of promoting him into a higher school or college, where the opportunities are richer, it has several disadvantages.

One disadvantage is that of giving the child a specious pre-
cocity, mainly verbal, without adequate backing in a variety of
experience in the areas where he might excel. It may produce a
good speller who knows the rules of grammar but has done no creative
writing and has not felt the stimulus of good literature creatively
taught. Or it may produce a boy who knows what the textbooks say
about chemistry and physics but has never worked "on his own" in a
laboratory.

Another disadvantage is that this kind of acceleration may prove
uninteresting to the child, since the curriculum itself is not interesting and is not enriched for him. Thus he may lose his motivation
to do good work.

Another serious problem of skipping is that it is often difficult to accelerate a child enough to provide for him intellectual
challenge without accelerating him into groups which are beyond his
physical, social, and emotional stages of development.

For these reasons grade-skipping has been opposed by many educators, who have attempted to meet the needs of talented children by
enrichment without speeding up their progress through school and
college.

Other methods of acceleration feature speedup or special progress
plans by which individuals or whole classes may complete work at a
faster pace than is usual. The difference between this and the "skipping" of grades is that the rate of progress is faster in the special
progress program, while in the skipping of grades the child moves
into a group at a higher level than that of his age-mates, but then
works at the pace of the new group, which is set by the average
students of that group.

In recent years there has been a trend toward a combination of
acceleration with enrichment which avoids most of the criticisms
aimed at simple grade-skipping. Therefore, several of the outstanding programs for gifted students now employ acceleration in the form
of special progress plans or early admission to college.

Acceleration as a school or college project.--The earliest possible point of acceleration is the first year of school. Bright
children may enter the kindergarten at age four or the first grade

at age five. Thus the accelerated child is always in school with a
group averaging a year older. Pittsburgh has arrangements for early
admission into school. A school may set up an accelerated program
for all its students, as does the University of Chicago Laboratory
School, which covers the usual eight years' work of elementary
school in seven years and thus graduates its students from high
school a year earlier than does the ordinary school. The program
of this school is one of enrichment, and the average I.Q. of its
students is about 125 or 130.

The New York City school system offers "special progress classes"
in 62 junior high schools for about 3,000 pupils. These classes complete the three-year junior high school program in two years and thus
enter senior high school with a year of acceleration. Baltimore has
two junior high schools in which bright pupils may do the work of
three years in two years' time. Careful consideration is given to
the physical-maturity level of children who are accelerated on this
plan.

Another transition point where time may be saved is between high
school and college. High-school students may be accepted in college
after they complete the eleventh grade in the Program for Early Admission to College, a current experiment by twelve colleges and
universities. Eleventh-grade students and even tenth-grade students
may be admitted to the colleges if they show sufficient academic
ability and personal maturity. During World War II there was a good
deal of acceleration into college after this pattern, and Pressey's
studies of the college careers of these students indicate that they
did not suffer academically or socially from their acceleration.[2]
Terman and Oden in their study of high-ability children concluded
that "children of 135 IQ or higher should be promoted sufficiently
to permit college entrance by the age of seventeen at latest and
that a majority in this group would be better off to enter at
sixteen."[3]

Another form of acceleration at the close of high school consists of admission to college with advanced standing earned by

---

[2]Sidney L. Pressey, Educational Acceleration: Appraisal and Basic
Problems, p. 153. Bureau of Educational Research Monographs, No.
31. Columbus: Ohio State University, 1949.

[3]L. M. Terman and Melita Oden, The Gifted Child Grows Up, p. 281.
Stanford University: Stanford University Press, 1947.

college-level work done in high school. The School and College Study
of Admission with Advanced Standing is carried on by a committee representing twelve secondary schools and twelve colleges. High-school
courses have been outlined in eleven subjects conventionally taught
to college Freshmen. These courses may be studied by high-school students in the tenth, eleventh, and twelfth grades, and they prepare
students for Sophomore-level work in college. Thus high-school students may earn as much as a year's college credit as part of their
four-year high-school program. Colleges will give credit to high-
school students for these college courses on the basis of examinations.

Both types of acceleration--early entrance to college and the
earning of college credit for work done in high school--are being
tried in the School and College Study of General Education, which is
a co-operative project of three preparatory schools--Andover, Exeter,
and Lawrenceville--with three universities--Princeton, Harvard, and
Yale.

Acceleration as an individual matter.--The skipping of grades has
always been a possibility for individuals in most school systems,
though too often this has not been accompanied by enrichment for the
child. Most educators believe that acceleration by one year is
satisfactory for a bright child who is physically and socially
advanced. Probably this practice is gaining slowly in approval by
educators. It is becoming more common in high school, through the
opportunities given by increasing numbers of colleges to superior
high-school students, either to enter college after the eleventh grade
of high school or to secure college credit for advanced high-school
courses.

CHAPTER VII

SUMMARIES OF PROGRAMS FOR GIFTED BOYS AND GIRLS

In the following pages we give summaries of the programs of about forty schools or other institutions which are doing especially interesting work with gifted children. These summaries are short and generally too scanty to do justice to the quality and quantity of work done in the schools mentioned; but they give some idea of its scope and variety.

We have undoubtedly missed some equally good places in this brief survey, and several very good schools did not answer our inquiries. Consequently, we are inclined to look at this chapter as an exhibit of what is being done in the places where the most interesting work is going on and to recognize the fact that a small number of public school systems and a considerable number of private schools might be found which offer as good programs as those reported in these pages.

The summaries are arranged alphabetically, by states, and some special projects, not located in any one community, are placed at the end of the list.

*

BIRMINGHAM PUBLIC SCHOOLS, BIRMINGHAM, ALABAMA

J. R. Obenchain, Director of the Guidance Department

*

The Birmingham public school system, organized on the eight-four plan, serves approximately 62,000 children in this industrial community of some 326,000 people. It provides a program for its superior children by means of special classes with an enriched curriculum and by individualized instruction in conventional classes. The officially organized special classes involve 110 children and 3 teachers in 2 elementary schools.

Candidates for special classes are selected from all schools in the city on the basis of teacher and principal recommendations, achievement-test results, physical condition, I.Q. of 120 or above, and parents' consent. Children are usually selected for these classes from the fifth grade of various schools and remain with the same enrichment teacher until they complete the eighth grade.

Enrichment class schedules fit into the platoon system on which the Birmingham schools are organized. The enrichment teacher has charge of two groups, each of which spends one-half day with her. During the other half of the day the students go to special-subject teachers, where they receive instruction in such subjects as art, auditorium, and playground.

The special classes are usually organized with class officers, sometimes as city governments. Students participate extensively in the planning and carrying-out of the class activities. Co-operative projects as well as individual work are featured. Pupils are allowed greater than the usual amount of freedom in class activities. Less emphasis is placed on grades and report cards. For example, some English activities of an enrichment class are the reading of poetry, stories, and articles that have to do with holidays; presentation of skits based on books read by groups in the class; quiz programs; class council meetings conducted entirely by the students; pupil interviews with various people of the community; and the writing of letters to various firms in the community to obtain permission for a class visit.

History is studied by the project method. After the selection of a topic, the class goes to the public library in a group and selects a subject of particular interest, does research, and writes a chapter for the class project record. Those gifted in art make illustrations for the cover.

Social studies, mathematics, spelling, and other regular subjects are also studied in the enrichment classes. In addition to the officially organized special classes, separate groups of superior children have been formed in some of the other schools as principals have seen the need arise.

Provision for superior children is also made in regular class-rooms, but the program is not so clearly defined as in the enrichment classes. Efforts are made, through special assignments, extracurri-cular activities, and the development of units of work, to provide the gifted child with a program that will keep him working at a pace commensurate with his abilities. In the larger schools, where there are enough first-graders for more than one teacher, the children are frequently grouped according to learning ability. In such cases the upper group receives an enriched curriculum.

In addition to visiting the museums, parks, airport, industrial plants, and banks of Birmingham, pupils of the enrichment classes take trips to other parts of the state, in particular to see the state capitol and the hydroelectric plants of the TVA.

* * *

NORTH PHOENIX HIGH SCHOOL, PHOENIX, ARIZONA
C. A. Brown, Department of Chemistry

*

North Phoenix High School is a four-year public high school with 2,500 students and a faculty of 100, located in Phoenix, an agricultu-ral and tourist center as well as the state capitol. Air Force instal-lations and manufacturing also play a large role in the local economy of this city of 250,000 people. The school offers a general program, in which about 65 students and 9 faculty members are engaged; it is designed to seek out students of superior ability, develop their poten-tial while in the school, and encourage them to enter scientific work as a career.

Students are identified and selected for this science program by means of previous school records, intelligence- and achievement-test results, and teachers' and counselors' recommendations.

All the science teachers, working with the school counselors and with the co-operation of the administration, plan this program for the gifted.

The work of the physics department is an example of this program. Students for the special physics class must have had three years of mathematics and be taking a fourth year and must have demonstrated their ability to do good work. The instructor's approval, after an individual conference, is also required for admission. Enrichment of the course is provided to students by using advanced material from special college texts and supplementary problems supplied by the instructor. Class lectures, demonstrations, and explanations feature more theoretical detail as well as higher mathematical concepts. The solutions to approximately three times as many problems are required as in an ordinary physics class.

As a part of the course, each member sets up a research problem,
plans the solution, and carries out the research. Reports of this
work are required to be well organized and properly presented from
the standpoints of English composition and scientific accuracy. Interest in the present progress of science and in the possibilities
for the future is developed through the reading of current literature.

The school also arranges for the science students to meet and
hear from many of the scientists of the community. Often these men
explain their research plans and demonstrate equipment.

Another feature of the school's program is its participation in
the Westinghouse Science Talent Search. One of the science teachers
sponsors the student activity in this nation-wide competition, in
which the school has been particularly successful.

* * *

WEST PHOENIX HIGH SCHOOL, PHOENIX, ARIZONA

Donald F. Stone, Principal

*

West Phoenix is a four-year public high school offering a general
program. The community in which it is located is largely suburban but
has within its boundaries some business, industrial, and agricultural
areas. The school enrolment is about 2,500, and this student population
is representative of the community, largely middle class. The program
for the gifted is integrated with the regular school activities as much
as possible and consists of guidance, enrichment in the regular classroom, some special classes, and a school-community co-operative program.

This school goes into the feeder elementary schools in the spring
of each year to give intelligence and achievement tests to the prospec-
tive Freshmen, to counsel, and to enrol them. At this time special
attention is given to the gifted child. He is identified through the
use of elementary-school records and the pre-Freshman program and is
then given the individual attention of a counselor, who helps him plan
his high-school work. Educational, vocational, and personal counseling
is also provided throughout the student's high-school career.

"Social Living" is an orientation course required of all Freshmen.
Taught by counselors, it is built around these units: the school program, safety education, community relations, and vocational-educational
planning. Group tests in the areas of ability, personality, and
interests are administered, interpreted, and charted on profiles during
the year. Individual tests and conferences are provided for the gifted
students.

In mathematics classes textbooks with graded exercises are used,
and extra-credit assignments are given. Gifted students are also
encouraged to come in after school for extra work in their regular
subjects or in college-level mathematics. Superior students are encouraged to check out advanced mathematics books for the summer. Semester

review outlines and study guides are furnished those students who plan
to take college board tests or scholarship examinations or enter competitions such as the Science Talent Search.

College-preparatory students are screened in the eighth grade,
and only the better students are encouraged to take algebra. Then
only the students who receive a high grade in that course are encouraged to take the more advanced courses. By reason of this selective
process, most of the students in the advanced courses are gifted and
are prepared to do work on a level comparable to that given in most
colleges for the Freshman year.

A world literature class is set up as a college preparatory
course and is recommended for students of superior ability. In this
class, classical backgrounds in literature are explored, vocabulary
studies made, and research papers written. A special group of superior
students in developmental reading strive to improve their reading speed
in all subjects. Other English classes offer extra projects or more-
advanced books for superior students.

In art, gifted students are encouraged to complete more projects
in class, particularly of the problem-solving variety, and are allowed
to work on projects after school. Gifted students act as foremen for
classes and help teach the slower students. They also help teachers
in their contact work with organizations in and out of school. Occasionally these students hold jobs outside school in the advertising
field or do artwork with civic and church organizations.

Other departments and classes offer similar opportunities for the
gifted.

Outstanding students from the business department go into community
offices and establishments to assume adult responsibilities for a half-
day in the second semester of their Senior year.

A career day for all students is also held each year, during which
time outstanding members of the community in various occupations and
professions co-operate with the school to assist in the vocational
orientation of students.

Another feature of the school program is a foreign student exchange
plan involving one boy and girl each year.

* * *

BERKELEY PUBLIC SCHOOLS, BERKELEY, CALIFORNIA

A. B. Campbell, Assistant Superintendent in
Charge of Educational Services

*

The public schools of Berkeley are a system of 14 elementary schools,
3 junior high schools, and 1 senior high school located in this San Francisco Bay city of 115,000 people. For the educational development of
gifted students these schools offer a program of enrichment in the regular

classroom, sectioned grades, and special activities in art and music.

In the junior and senior high schools academic classes are homogeneous for the most part. This grouping has its inception in the elementary schools, where the sixth-grade teachers, making use of intelligence-test scores, standardized-test results, and teachers' judgments over the preceding several years, recommend into which seventh-grade section each child will go. Junior high school counselors, working with the teachers, occasionally modify this judgment.

The ninth-grade counselor, working with the student, makes out a tenth-grade program which is sent home for the parents' approval. This procedure usually results in the student's being placed in classes with others of like interests and ability. Enrichment in these and other regular classes is offered by the individual teacher.

The talented music student, whether he intends to pursue music as an avocation or as a vocation, has many opportunities available to him in the Berkeley schools. Provision is made at the elementary level for excellence in instrumental music by the organization of an All-City Orchestra which meets outside school and plays music of a more challenging type than would be possible at the local school level. In the choral field, glee clubs have been organized in practically all the schools. Classroom teachers often encourage members of these groups by arranging for individual performances.

There is also an All-City Orchestra at the junior high school level, and each school has a boys' and girls' glee club. Talent shows are presented, and the school music teachers work with the classroom teacher to provide opportunities for members to perform before their classmates.

At the senior high school level, orchestra, band, and swing band afford opportunities for the student excelling in instrumental music. For the serious vocal student there is the A Capella Choir. Classes in harmony and composition are offered, and creative work is presented in an annual concert. A music club prepares concerts. Annual talent shows perform for radio and television audiences, service clubs, churches, and other community organizations. Activities in other departments of the high school are carried on for the benefit of the gifted. Students in the science club, in addition to keeping up many individual projects, compete for participation in the Science Fair held annually in Berkeley. A Speakers' Club is active in stimulating school and community interest on the part of service clubs and other groups in the United Crusade, the Red Cross, conservation, and other community activities.

The Berkeley Music Council and the Victor Schott Memorial Fund furnish scholarships to outstanding students at the elementary and junior high school level for work during the summer in music workshops and summer camps.

Under the sponsorship of the P.T.A. and the Berkeley schools, each year the San Francisco Symphony Orchestra gives a series of four concerts during the school day. Talented children who would not otherwise be able to attend are given free tickets by the P.T.A.

The community also co-operates with the schools in a program of special art classes. One of these classes, sponsored by the Art League of the East Bay, meets one day a week after school during the school year. A summer art class for children meets each morning for the first six weeks of the summer vacation. A junior high school furnishes the room for this class, and the California College of Arts and Crafts selects the teachers.

* * *

LOS ANGELES CITY ELEMENTARY SCHOOLS, LOS ANGELES 12, CALIFORNIA

Donald J. Kincaid, Supervisor of Guidance and Counseling

*

The Los Angeles city elementary schools operate an experimental Special Work Program for Rapid Learners. This program is primarily one of separation for enrichment and involves 2 special teachers, in two centrally located schools, and about 100 students gathered from 24 of the 374 schools that serve the 255,000 school children of the city. These 100 pupils consist of groups of 12-15, who meet one morning a week with their Special Work Program teacher.

Selection of a pupil for the Special Work Program is based on regular grade placement of fourth, fifth, or sixth grades, I.Q. of 130 or above (usually from an individual test), high achievement-test scores, enrolment in a school within easy access to one of the special schools, approval of principal and regular teacher, consent of parents, and interest shown by the child.

A number of standardized group tests and especially designed questionnaires are administered to the pupils who participate in the Special Work Program: the advanced form of the Stanford Achievement Test, the Calvert Science Information Test, the Iowa Work Study Skills Test, the Lee-Thorpe Occupational Interest Inventory, the California Test of Personality, the "About Myself" Questionnaire, a teachers' check list, and sociometric tests. The purpose of these measures is to aid the teacher in planning class procedures and providing materials for pupil activities and to explore the use of these tests as possible tools for evaluating the program.

A number of activities take place in the special-class groups. Emphasis is given to the exploration and use of many types of conference material. Books are furnished by the city schools and the Los Angeles public libraries. New books are added at least once a month. The writing of autobiographies, original stories, and poems furnishes experience in creative writing. Class discussions provide opportunity for the learning of discussion techniques. As the written and oral expressions of the pupils are observed, instructional and remedial activities in the language arts are provided.

Science activities include varied reading, performance of simple experiments, individual studies in some chosen area, and a visit to the

annual Science Fair at the Los Angeles County Museum. Geography includes globe study, map-projection study, and pictorial mapmaking.
Children are encouraged to bring their hobby collections to class and
share their experiences. French and Spanish are studied as they relate to class activities. Civics features concern governmental
problems suited to the age level, such as "How shall our flag be re-
designed if Alaska and Hawaii become states?"

Study of the use of money includes the sensible use of personal
allowances and what souvenirs to buy on a trip. Arithmetic activities
include the study of the history of numbers, other number and measuring
systems, additional denominate number work, deriving formulas, making
graphs, and drawing to scale. In art the children study design, color,
arrangement, notebook-making, and diorama and puppet craft.

Another phase of the Special Work Program for Rapid Learners is
the library class. Senior members of the special groups are invited to
join this library class, which meets about twice a month at the down-
town Los Angeles City Library. Activities include learning how to use
the card catalogue, use of the magazine guides, experience in a model
library, learning discrimination in choosing books to read or buy, using
the map section and the audio-visual department. Under the immediate
direction of the children's librarian, each lesson is based on the
interests of the students. Each meeting brings a special book, a magazine article, an idea to pursue, or a new reference for each child,
whether that child's interest is in aviation, nature study, adventure
stories, horses, or biography.

* * *

LOS ANGELES CITY SECONDARY SCHOOLS, LOS ANGELES 12, CALIFORNIA

G. Millage Montgomery, Associate Superintendent

*

The Los Angeles city secondary schools are a group of 86 junior
and senior high schools attended by some 141,000 students. Individual
schools adopt programs for their gifted students to meet the varying
needs of the students and the communities they live in, so that no
completely uniform practice exists throughout the city. However, the
basic city-wide sectioning policy is to form a top group for each area
of academic work. In some instances these classes are composed of
only the academically gifted pupils. In other cases a differentiated
curriculum within the classes is necessary to meet the needs of the
superior students. Enrichment is emphasized throughout, whether in
special or in regular classes.

Group intelligence tests and a battery of achievement tests are
given every two years. After each period of testing, listings are made
of those students in the ninetieth percentile and above in intelligence
and composite achievement. Data are also analyzed to point out specific
needs of the gifted, and listings are made of those who are deficient,
those who are average, and those who are superior in a particular area

of achievement. This information is directed to school principals,
along with suggestions for the programs of the gifted students. A
letter is also sent to the parents of those who achieve in the top
10 per cent of city students.

Although each school may vary its procedures, certain enrichment
practices are common. In the area of science, classes are sometimes
designed to cover the requirements of two semesters' work in one
semester. Club activities are co-ordinated with classroom work.
Opportunities are provided for gifted students to explore particular
interests as deeply as mathematical backgrounds permit, to use research methods of a more searching type, and to demonstrate experiments
to classes. The difference between science and technology is studied.
Participation in approved local and national contests is encouraged,
as are independent trips to museums, laboratories, and observatories.

In the language arts, gifted students are encouraged to do more
choosing, planning, and evaluating of their own learning activities.
They may read independently in areas of special interest and write
original stories and plays for class or school publications, for local
papers, or simply for enjoyment. Language skills are evaluated
through the use of a tape recorder. Ethical problems are discussed,
using texts as points of departure, and studies are made of Latin and
Greek roots to words. Gifted students may be appointed to summarize
and record class plans. They are also encouraged to enter contests
and to make independent trips to newspaper and printing offices, book-
stores, and libraries.

Similar enrichment procedures are employed in the areas of social
studies and mathematics.

Scholarship chairmen are appointed in many of the high schools of
the system, and scholarship opportunities are developed with the co-
operation of industrial and business concerns of the community. Some
work experience is offered in fields of special ability and interest.

University and technical representatives from the community are
invited to discuss vocational opportunities with students and their
parents. Leaders in the community may sponsor the individual projects
of gifted students. The school program is also co-ordinated with such
activities as the annual Science Fair at the County Museum.

* * *

SAN DIEGO CITY SCHOOLS, SAN DIEGO 3, CALIFORNIA

Ralph Dailard, Superintendent of Schools

*

San Diego, a Pacific Coast city of 415,000 people, has a system
of 67 elementary, 8 junior high, and 7 regular secondary schools serving
about 64,000 students. In the elementary schools, gifted pupils receive
enrichment in the regular classroom, with some acceleration in individual
cases. In the secondary schools they receive enrichment in the regular

classroom or may be released from the normal course of study sequence to take special classes.

A city-wide screening program provides that a teacher or principal may recommend a child for a Binet intelligence test. This recommendation may be based on observation, grades, or group intelligence-, aptitude-, or achievement-test scores. Siblings of gifted students are also tested. Those scoring three standard deviations or more above the mean on the individual intelligence test (usually 148 or more) are defined as gifted.

Parents of the children selected for special treatment are notified and interviewed. This contact is supplemented by progress report meetings held twice annually. Parents are also encouraged to initiate consultations.

Each school principal directs the work in his school, assisted by 4 teacher consultants for gifted children, a visiting teacher, and his school psychologist. A special class has been established for maladjusted gifted pupils on the elementary level. On the secondary level special counseling and guidance are given to help gifted students prepare for college and obtain scholarships. On both levels priority is given to these students for psychological or visiting teacher help.

Gifted children in the regular elementary grades are given creative work to do in the place of what would for them be needless, dull assignments. They may spend only from one to three periods a week, instead of the usual five, on spelling from the state text. The released time is used for creative writing. In all subject-matter areas the work is enriched. In a social studies unit, for example, the gifted use a greater number of reference books and more difficult ones. They are assigned problems and questions that require a high degree of critical thinking. They assume responsibility for a greater number of projects and for more involved ones in connection with the unit. Spare-time activities are keyed to existing or potential interests. Superior pupils may produce a puppet play, carry on foreign correspondence, perform scientific experiments, build a radio or telegraph set, or work in some art medium not included in the course of study at their grade levels. In all these activities the regular classroom teacher is assisted by the teaching consultants provided by the program.

Acceleration of elementary pupils is limited and depends on physical, social, and educational maturity.

The work in mathematics is a good example of how the gifted are treated in the secondary schools. Able students do seventh- and eighth-grade work in the seventh grade. Eighth-grade students use ninth-grade books. Ninth-grade students go into an advanced mathematics class. Considerable emphasis is placed on games, puzzles, and other mathematics applications. Puzzle contests from the Oklahoma University Mathematics Newsletter are used. Work with calculating machines, computers, slide rules, logarithms, and other devices and topics is introduced early.

In English classes, as another example of the treatment of the gifted on the secondary level, standard-test scores are used to determine the level of need, and work is assigned accordingly. In some cases pupils are accelerated into higher classes. Talented students are encouraged to enrol in debate, public speaking, and drama. Advanced English courses offer extensive reading, critical evaluation of books, script-writing (occasionally for a local educational television show), extensive use of literary magazines, and participation in essay contests.

In all departments, if a student can demonstrate prior mastery of a subject by passing an examination in it, he may then be released from certain of the required courses to take electives of his own choice.

The San Diego program also uses various community resources. Citizens are members of the steering committee that plans the special curriculum. Resource persons from the community speak to classes. War-surplus electronic materials have been donated to school shops and laboratories. Students participate in the local Science Fair. Classes make local visits. For example, an art class visits the art gallery each month for a planned series of studies, and students interested in astronomy go to the Mount Palomar and Griffith observatories.

* * *

EVANSTON TOWNSHIP HIGH SCHOOL, EVANSTON, ILLINOIS

L. S. Michael, Superintendent

*

Evanston Township High School is a four-year, comprehensive public high school located in a favored suburban city near Chicago. It has an enrolment of 2,460 and employs 156 faculty members. About 75 per cent of its students go on to institutions of higher learning upon graduation. The program it provides its most gifted students is a broad one, involving about 25 per cent of the student body and a third of the faculty. Its purpose is to identify and develop talent; and it features a project for the improvement of thinking, an honors program, active participation in the Westinghouse Science Talent Search, participation in the School and College Study of Admission with Advanced Standing, an affiliation with the Horace Mann-Lincoln Institute Study of Talented Youth, and an unusually rich and well-planned co-curricular program. Classes for gifted students are generally small and homogeneous, but use is also made of regular class groupings of mixed ability. Limited acceleration is provided. The curriculum is generally enriched by the addition of more advanced activities with more comprehensive range.

Teachers' judgments, intelligence- and achievement-test scores, and information on reading habits, vocational plans, and hobbies are used to identify gifted students. With the co-operating institute's resources and through systematic study, the school hopes to gain a better understanding of the meaning of superior talent and to determine possible curriculum modifications by which schools can improve their provisions for identifying and developing talent. Of real concern is the search for scientific evidence to the value of curricular changes.

The project for the improvement of thinking is carried out jointly with two neighboring high schools and in co-operation with the Illinois Curriculum Program. It involves giving a new emphasis to semantics, logic, and methods of inquiry and justification in units of work in English, mathematics, science, and social studies. Eight of the thirty classes in this project are designated as honors sections, for especially gifted students.

Encouragement is given to gifted students to participate in science fairs and enter science competitions, particularly the Westinghouse Talent Search. The special science curriculum features acceleration for those qualified. Talented students by-pass ninth-grade general science and enter directly the tenth-grade biology class. This is followed by progression through chemistry, physics, and possibly a science seminar for those who qualify. Besides the individual laboratory projects, these courses include extensive reading of scientific literature, particularly of research reports in areas of interest. The development of scientific attitudes and methods are emphasized, and teachers in all classes try to point out the application of scientific principles to practical social and economic problems.

As a pilot school of the Admission to College with Advanced Standing Study, the school offers certain courses on an advanced level for select students. In the advanced English course, for example, the first part of the semester is devoted to student weaknesses in literary background, critical analysis, impromptu writing, outlining, and organization. Time is then devoted to creative writing for contests, particularly the Atlantic and Scholastic competitions. Work is done with short-short stories, short stories, formal and informal essays, and verse. Personal interviews with the students also play an important part in the course.

The college-level European history course offers a program of wide reading characterized by analysis, interpretation, and criticism of the principal events, periods, institutions, and ideas of Western civilization. Students give written and oral reports which emphasize these procedures. Class discussion follows the Socratic method.

College-level science will offer a second year of study in physics or chemistry to the gifted, while college-level mathematics will introduce them to differential and integral calculus and analytics.

Illustrative of the exceptionally profitable experiences available in the nearly fifty co-curricular activities are the small and selective Mastersingers, along with the massive and impressive festival choruses performing with full orchestra, the Central Council giving leadership roles to fifty in an active organization of over three

hundred, and the girls' leaders program which provides advanced and
special class training enabling the gifted in physical education
almost entirely to direct the G.A.A. program.

* * *

NEW TRIER TOWNSHIP HIGH SCHOOL, WINNETKA, ILLINOIS

R. H. Carpenter, Assistant Superintendent

*

New Trier Township High School serves several favored suburban
communities near Chicago. In a school of about 2,600 students and
160 faculty members, almost 50 per cent of the faculty and students
engage in some form of work for talented students. The school has
no "special" program for its gifted students, but through its enriched
curriculum and varied activities it offers opportunities for the development of its superior students in many directions. This program
provides for students of high intelligence, students gifted in the
field of leadership, and those with special talents.

In the academic field, students in the upper fifth of their
class, on the basis of intelligence-test scores, estimates of teachers,
evidence of health and leadership, and patterns of conduct, register
in classes of enriched instruction in English, mathematics, language,
and history.

At the Freshman level an integrated course in English, science,
and history for the academically gifted enrols about 10 per cent of
the entering class. A Sophomore course combines in one period the
teaching of English and history.

In the upper years of the school there is less direct segregation, but the school offers subjects on an advanced level which
normally appeal only to the especially interested or gifted student.
The fourth year of English provides courses in world literature, the
great books, advanced dramatics, debate, and public speaking.

The mathematics department embraces four and one-half years'
work, carrying through trigonometry and college algebra. The science
department offers courses in chemistry and physics. Electives in
senior history provide for the study of economics, advanced civics
and government, sociology, the history of Latin America, and the
history of the Far Eastern areas. Final years of the foreign-language
courses are designed for especially able students.

New Trier offers a number of activities, formerly called "extracurricular" but now incorporated into the regular program, which
provide opportunities for the development of leadership. The Student
Council accepts a large measure of responsibility. Under its direction
students supervise and operate most of the study halls. Council
leaders have also developed a classroom honor system, in which nearly

every class in the school participates. An all-school boys' club
and an all-school girls' club take major responsibilities in various
areas of school activity. Such positions as those held by club officers, athletic managers, leads in the annual opera or in the student
talent show, all provide additional opportunities for leadership.

The school develops special talent in other than the purely academic fields by providing for specialization in these fields far
beyond the needs of the average student. In art, for example, it is
possible for the New Trier student to spend four years in study and
to develop many different types of artistic expression. The art department uses the walls of corridors and classrooms for exhibits of
current work by Chicago artists and develops contacts with the Chicago
Art Institute. The music department conducts about sixteen different
choral groups of varying degrees of efficiency. Bands and orchestras
provide instrumental experience, and it is possible for talented
students to study and take private lessons during free periods at
school. Christmas and spring concerts involve over a thousand
students and offer solo experience for the talented. The annual
light opera provides musical experience at a high level of artistic
performance.

Courses in laboratory and special fields provide additional opportunities. Two examples of this are in the fields of radio and
photography, where students attain a proficiency seldom achieved
except by the professional.

* * *

FRANCIS W. PARKER SCHOOL, 330 WEBSTER AVENUE, CHICAGO 14, ILLINOIS

Herbert W. Smith, Principal

*

Francis W. Parker is a coeducational private school from kindergarten through the twelfth grade, located favorably on the Near North
Side of Chicago. Scholarships and the cosmopolitan location of the
school contribute to making the student body representative of many
economic and cultural groups. Practically all the graduates go on to
college. In this school about 45 teachers and 450 students participate
in a program which, though not making special provisions for gifted
children, offers opportunity for their development by reason of the
quality of the staff and equipment, the enriched curriculum, the small
classes, and the attention to individual needs and interests.

All children in the school are given at least two standard intelligence tests. Most high-school students take college board tests.
Rorschach and Thematic Apperception Tests are given when it is thought
that they may be useful for purposes of guidance, placement, and
teaching.

The concept of the gifted child held at this school is an inclu-
sive one. It may pertain to those gifted in academic subjects,

athletics, drama, music, student government, work with young children, social sensitivity, or other areas. As gifted children evidence themselves in the classroom, teachers attempt to enrich their program. This effort consists typically of encouraging them both to broaden their interests and to engage in some special project in their line of interest that will benefit the whole class. Sometimes these students are used directly to help teach others.

The school provides a variety of experiences--classwork, independent study, exercise, play, and group projects. Effort is made to discover the special aptitudes of each child and, through the use of varied equipment, to provide means for expression. It offers the all-day program of a country day school, with playgrounds, gardens, and pets at hand, as well as museums, shops, and theaters, and the life of a large city. Small classes give time and freedom to work with each child.

Subjects are correlated, wherever possible, through co-operation between subject departments. Students are taught to see that physics and chemistry alike are related to zoology; that drama and psychology are related; that history, geography, economics, politics, and sociology are all related. The sequence of courses is considered flexible, and plans are often changed to accommodate current interests.

Parker School also provides a continuous progression of experiences in the nonacademic fields of the arts. All students are scheduled for art, crafts, music, and drama classes appropriate to the level of advancement.

Observing, doing, and making are stressed in laboratories, in shops, and on field trips. Students go on as many as thirty trips a year, to museums, mills, stores, concerts, farms, churches, housing projects, courts, the sand dunes, and other places of education and amusement. A firsthand knowledge of and familiarity with things are seen as important stimuli to original and creative thinking and a sound basis for later specialized study.

* * *

QUINCY PUBLIC SCHOOLS, QUINCY, ILLINOIS

L. O. Litle, Superintendent of Schools

*

The Quincy Public Schools serve a city of 43,000, with approximately 400 children in each grade level of the elementary schools. The program for gifted children is being conducted in collaboration with the Quincy Youth Development Commission and with several community organizations which are interested in gifted children. The program has been initiated in the elementary schools, mainly through enrichment in the regular classrooms. The junior high school will soon be involved, and probably the senior high school will be brought into the program later.

The Quincy schools attempt to discover ways and means of providing:

1. An enrichment program in areas of the school curriculum for all children, with particular emphasis upon an enrichment program for children with special talents or exceptional ability
2. Special educational opportunities in both the school and the community for the 1 or 2 per cent of pupils that are truly "gifted"

Identification of talented children is carried through by a system of tests of various sorts at the primary grades and higher levels, backed by teachers' nominations. The experimental work on identification was done with the aid of the Youth Development Commission. At present a "Teachers Identification Handbook" is being devised as a guide to teachers in discovering and working with talented children. A wide variety of talent is being searched for, including talent in art, music, creative writing, and social leadership.

The program for gifted children is being developed by a study group known as the "Curriculum Enrichment Committee," which consists of 10 classroom teachers from Grades III through VIII, 3 elementary principals, an elementary curriculum director, and the superintendent of schools. This committee has been directly responsible for the work of this project. All interested teachers have been encouraged to contribute ideas and materials to the program. The study-group members will become consultants and resource persons for summer workshops, preschool conferences, and in-service training programs.

Enrichment procedures developed by this committee are reported back to the elementary schools. At the same time, the committee has asked each teacher in the elementary schools to select one gifted child in her class and to make a special study of this child and of ways to help him develop his particular abilities.

Community agencies are being encouraged to work with talented youth. An outstanding example is the program conducted by the YWCA on Saturday mornings for girls and boys of elementary-school age, which includes a painting class and a dramatics group.

* * *

UNIVERSITY OF CHICAGO LABORATORY SCHOOLS, UNIVERSITY OF CHICAGO, CHICAGO 37, ILLINOIS

Lloyd Urdal, Principal

*

The Laboratory Schools of the University of Chicago are private demonstration and experimental schools located on the university campus. The combined enrolment of the kindergarten, lower school, and upper school is about 800, and the full- and part-time faculty numbers about 80. Forty per cent of the students come from faculty homes. The majority of the others are the children of professional and business people. The Laboratory Schools have no special program for their superior students

but, by reason of the caliber of students admitted and the nature of
the curriculum, may be considered to be operating an enriched and accelerated program for gifted children.

Students are admitted after consideration of intelligence- and
achievement-test results, consideration of reports from previous
schools, evaluation of social and emotional adjustment, observation,
and interviews with parents. Each candidate must give promise of
being able to meet the standards achieved by those students already
in the schools. The average I.Q. of those admitted is about 130.

Various means are used to challenge students to do their best.
Effort is made to relate activities to present needs, and field trips,
laboratory, and studio work help build new interests. Activities are
related to meaningful purposes, such as in the mastering of spelling
words in order to present a discussion to classmates rather than
learning the first group of words of a prepared list. Further, the
variety of topics and problems which are studied in the curriculum
helps stimulate interest and ambition.

The work of individual students is varied somewhat to suit their
particular characteristics, and they are offered a number of ways to
reach desired goals. Competition is not emphasized. Individuals are
rated against themselves up to the high-school level. In the high-
school grades a student is rated against his peers. Achievement in
all school objectives, academic and otherwise, is recorded at regular
intervals by means of a standardized testing program.

The central educational objective of the schools is to help the
students better to solve their contemporary and future problems. Accordingly, the curriculum presents a wide variety of appropriate
problem experiences and tries to offer opportunities for students to
learn to think about them with a command of the necessary facts and
other knowledge. The regular academic work is a part of these experiences. The upper-school homerooms--in which academic, social, and
personal questions are discussed; the "showing and telling time" of
the kindergartens; the dramatics activities of the middle grades; the
beginners' orchestra; and the after-school club activities are
examples of other experiences. Added to this are the activities provided by the well-equipped laboratories, studios, shops, gymnasium,
and the facilities of the university.

Classes are ordinarily heterogeneous. Each grade has three sections, but they are comparable. The maximum size of each group is
twenty-five. For the regular academic program, each class is divided
into groups which concentrate on tehir own needs in the subject. Work
assignments are differentiated, and additional assignments are given
to some groups. Special teachers are provided for the unified arts
program of home arts, shop, art, dramatics, and music. The last period
of each day is a conference hour, during which time students may work
with teachers for enrichment or remedial attention in academic matters,
or they may confer with their advisers about school problems.

Although the program offered the students is basically one of
enrichment, a type of acceleration is provided, in that eight years of

regular public school work are covered in the first seven years of the Laboratory Schools. After completing the eleventh year, the graduate is then ready to enter college. Preparation for college is a major concern of the schools.

Resources outside the schools are used in various ways as they supplement units of study in the classroom. Being affiliated with the university makes available such facilities as the Audio-Visual Aids Center and the Reading Clinic. Members of the university faculty give talks and present demonstrations. The city of Chicago also provides many educational resources in the way of museums, zoos, parks, factories, stores, and theaters. Frequent trips to these places are related to classroom experiences, as when a lower-school class visits the zoo after a unit of study on the ground hog or an upper-school English class sees Macbeth. As a special school feature, each spring the sixth grade spends a week at a summer camp, where learning activities are related to science and conservation studies.

* * *

INDIANAPOLIS PUBLIC ELEMENTARY SCHOOLS, INDIANAPOLIS, INDIANA

Jeanette Riker, Supervisor of Special Education

*

The public schools of Indianapolis include a group of 84 elementary schools. A program for the gifted of these schools is offered in eight special classes, covering Grades V, VI, VII, and VIII, located in 7 schools in various sections of the city. These classes serve 205 pupils drawn from about 60 different schools. The purpose of the program is to promote the maximum growth of students of superior ability, without accelerating them beyond their age and social levels. To accomplish this, enrichment is offered in the areas of language arts, mathematics, science, and social studies; and activities are provided to develop good work and study habits, promote qualities of leadership, and raise the levels of appreciation in the fine arts. Although the pupils of this program are in special classes, every effort is made to include them as a part of the regular program of the school in which they are located.

All pupils in the Indianapolis schools are given group intelligence tests at the IA, IVB, and VIIB levels. Pupils new to the city are also tested. Those having an I.Q. of 125 or above may be referred for individual testing, depending on teachers' and principals' recommendations regarding their ability and achievement. Parents are also interviewed by the special education supervisor and by the school principals. Final recommendations for placement are made by the school psychologists.

Meetings are held with parents several times a year in each school, to discuss class organization and procedures and special problems.

For mathematics activities, the pupils in the special classes are pretested and placed in groups according to ability. Drill on skills is

done on an individual basis or in small groups, and periods of drill
are short and intensive. A limited amount of homework is assigned
in workbooks, for review. Emphasis is placed on mental arithmetic,
estimating answers, and rapid computation, particularly using round
numbers. Insofar as textbooks are used, they are adapted to the
needs of the gifted by eliminating needless explanatory and drillwork.
Practical applications of the arithmetic processes are made, and discussions analyzing a variety of socially and personally significant
problems are held. Graphs and tables are made for social studies and
science work, and charts are kept of individual progress and class
averages.

In science periods, effort is made to develop problem-solving
skill and a scientific way of thinking. Science is taught as related
to the regular interests and activities of life. The incidental
science interests of the children are supplemented and organized; and
causes, effects, and relationships are explored. This is accomplished
by means of extensive reading, discussion, reports, films, firsthand
observation, demonstration, experimentation, field trips, exhibits,
and construction activities.

In social studies the problem-solving approach is used. From the
course of study a large area is chosen for a problem. The problem is
then divided into units, and procedures are planned. The children may
work individually, in committees, as an entire class, or through a
combination of these. In these groups the students itemize what they
want to know and where to find this information. After material has
been collected, it is analyzed and accepted or rejected. The resulting
information is then organized and communicated to all those concerned.

In the language arts, standards are set up co-operatively. Both
individual and groupwork is featured in the various activities designed
to teach the techniques of research; promote interest in current events;
help make distinctions between fact and opinion; develop poise and self-
confidence before an audience; develop leadership; teach correct
English usage, spelling, and penmanship; and develop skill in social,
business-letter, and creative writing. Class activities include drama,
extensive reading, writing of book reports, choral speaking, periods of
sharing of stories and poetry, and clubwork.

Field trips are made to museums, parks, and stores. Speakers and
other programs are occasionally brought from the community to the
school. At various times students in the special classes participate
in such community projects as fund-raising campaigns and cleanup drives.

Scholarships provided by the Junior League of Indianapolis and the
Indianapolis Foundation have enabled teachers of the groups to receive
special training in work with gifted children.

* * *

* * *

THOMAS CARR HOWE HIGH SCHOOL, INDIANAPOLIS, INDIANA

C. M. Sharp, Principal

*

Thomas Carr Howe High School is part of the Indianapolis public school system. It is a four-year general high school with an enrolment of over 1,400 and a faculty of 70. About 50 per cent of the school's graduates go to college. The community it serves is located near the eastern outskirts of Indianapolis and is one of moderate income level. The program that this school offers its gifted attempts to provide the maximum amount of educational opportunities for them through enrichment of the curriculum, some homogeneous grouping, some acceleration in classes that prepare for advanced standing in college, and special major departmental guidance. The program includes all departments of the school to some extent, but particularly science and mathematics.

To identify candidates for the program, previous grade records are first examined. I.Q. scores of 115 or more and American Council on Education Test scores in the upper 10 per cent serve to identify others. Teachers are also polled for information. The Gifted Child Committee of the school, representing all academic departments, then prepares special brochures on each of the students selected.

Chosen students are interviewed by the committee, and each one is encouraged to find a teacher in his chosen field who will act as his adviser, not only in academic and vocational matters, but as a sponsor for a project to be pursued during his high-school career.

In the mathematics department, as in most of the departments, provision is made for gifted students in all classes by means of differentiated assignments, special projects, and outside reading. Special classes are offered in algebra, geometry, and advanced mathematics.

The science curriculum consists of biology, chemistry, and physics. There is no ninth-grade science course; so after one semester in the unsegregated tenth-grade biology course, the upper 10 per cent is chosen for the special second-semester biology course. This segregation continues, largely in the biology, chemistry, and physics classes that follow.

The advanced biology, physics, and chemistry courses are connected with the School and College Study for Admission with Advanced Standing and offer acceleration; but enrichment is the basic procedure in the classes for the gifted. This enrichment may take the form of special speakers (professors, physicians, technicians, other local professional people, and other members of the school faculty), special field trips (to universities, hospitals, industry, and museums), more experimental work, individual projects, lectures on the current developments in scientific theory and practice, the reading of advanced books, or extensive use of audio-visual materials. Students are also encouraged to enter and are coached for science contests, fairs, and competitions.

The school also makes use of the community's resources in the form of science equipment, publications, and audio-visual materials let to it by local institutions.

* * *

CEDAR RAPIDS PUBLIC SCHOOLS, CEDAR RAPIDS, IOWA

Leroy Peterson, Director of the Department of Special Education

*

The Cedar Rapids school system comprises 19 elementary and 4 junior-senior high schools. The city contains many large and small industries and has a population of about 78,000 and a school district of some 85,000 people. In the experimental school program for mentally advanced pupils, approximately 22 teachers work with about 100 children of Grades IV, V, and VI in two elementary schools and Grades VII and XI of one junior-senior high school. The program is primarily one of enrichment, emphasizing academic skills, and is geared to the gifted pupil on an individual basis in the regular classroom.

This special attention is confined to those students who have an I.Q. of 130 or more, as determined by an individual intelligence test administered by the Department of Special Education. Teachers refer to this department all students whose behavior in class, achievement-test scores, and group-test I.Q.'s indicate that they are mentally advanced. After the administration of an individual intelligence test indicates that a student is qualified for the program, a staff conference and a conference with the parents are held to consider the social, personal, and academic status of the child and to plan the program that will best meet his needs.

No effort is made to segregate the gifted for instructional purposes. The program is designed to enrich the experience of the student through individual attention in the regular classroom. A detailed report containing information about interests, abilities, achievement, and the social and emotional adjustment of each mentally advanced pupil in her room is supplied to the teacher. On the basis of this report each teacher with gifted children attempts to provide broader and more advanced experiences for them in the academic areas of mathematics, science, language arts, and social studies. One teacher spends full time working with the enrichment class teachers, helping them to secure suitable books and other materials.

A bulletin has also been published, giving specific suggestions for activities and techniques for use with mentally advanced pupils. This local publication and texts by professionals in the field of the education of the gifted are provided each teacher.

During social studies periods in the classroom, for example, gifted students take the lead in various activities. They collect travel folders for countries being studied, do research for murals or model constructions, and present original dramatizations of customs and historical events. Letters are exchanged with correspondents in foreign countries. Reports are given concerning current world and national topics, as well as events in which the students themselves have participated.

In mathematics, as another example, superior students do work in supplementary texts, covering the history of mathematics, problems drawn from daily living or suggested by science and social studies, and mathematics tricks and puzzles. Learning how to use such devices as the protractor and compass is also a part of the enrichment activities, as well as any extra drillwork that gifted students might feel the need to do.

Because the fourth, fifth, and sixth grades of the Cedar Rapids elementary schools have specially trained teachers in art, music, and physical education, talents and aptitudes in these areas are at present the responsibility of these special teachers.

The program in the one co-operating secondary school is for those students who have been earlier in the elementary program and have entered the seventh grade of this school.

* * *

ATCHISON PUBLIC SCHOOLS, ATCHISON, KANSAS
Charles W. Lafferty, Superintendent

*

The Atchison public schools are a group of 5 grade schools, with about 250 pupils per school, and a six-year high school, with a student body of 1,000. Atchison is a city of 13,000 people, located in an agricultural, milling, and industrial area, about 45 miles north of Kansas City. The needs of the gifted children in the elementary grades are provided for through enrichment of the work in the regular classrooms and through limited individual acceleration. A special feature planned for this program is a sixth-grade class for exceptional pupils from all parts of the city. On the secondary level, the program for the gifted is primarily one of guidance.

Gifted children are identified by means of intelligence tests and teachers' observations. Pinter-Cunningham group tests are administered at the kindergarten level, and the Kuhlmann-Finch test at the end of the second grade. At these times all those with I.Q.'s of 125 and above are chosen for special attention. In the third grade, all pupils receive an individual Binet, at which time 120 is a qualifying score. At all grade levels, faculty members watch for children with special abilities of any kind, and, upon recommendation, more refined examinations are made.

To supervise the program of the gifted children, a permanent committee has been established consisting of two administrative personnel,

two high-school teachers, and two grade-school teachers. This committee studies the children during the time they are in the public
schools and after their graduation and keeps a cumulative record for
each one. Meetings are held at various times, most often on Saturday.
Members are paid for the extra time, and secretarial help and office
space are provided for their work.

Representatives of the committee contact each teacher that has
a child in her class with an I.Q. of above 130. This contact is
continued throughout the school year, during which time the representative advises and assists the classroom teacher in enriching the
program of the exceptional child by providing him additional and more
varied opportunities for study, research, and meaningful experience.

Teachers having children with I.Q.'s of 120 to 130 in their
classrooms are notified by letter or memorandum. Individual contacts
are made only about once a year in these cases.

The committee also advises teachers and principals concerning
family contacts, parent-teacher conferences, and home visitations.

Some of the gifted are accelerated after consideration of educational, social, emotional, and physical maturity and their own
parents' wishes. This movement is facilitated by the arrangement of
having several combinatiin rooms (i.e., first and second grades, third
and fourth grades, fourth and fifth grades) in every elementary-school
building. At the third-grade level, gifted children are moved into a
fourth-grade room but remain as third-graders. Later, they enter the
fourth-and-fifth-grade room as fourth-graders. This process is
repeated in similar manner until they become sixth-graders.

Beginning in the fall of 1956, outstanding sixth-graders from all
schools of the city will be brought together in a special class which
will receive instruction advanced beyond that of the regular sixth
grade but not overlapping the work of the seventh-grade classes. At
the end of the sixth grade, some of the special students will be
advanced to the eighth grade, while the rest will go into the regular
seventh grade. It will then be possible for either group to accelerate
a maximum of one more year by carrying a heavier load during the remainder of the time that they are in high school.

At the secondary level, the gifted child committee assists the
high-school guidance personnel in making recommendations for the programs of the special students.

* * *

CHILDRENS' SUMMER STUDIO, LAWRENCE RECREATION COUNCIL,
LAWRENCE, KANSAS

John Garcia, Supervisor of Art, Lawrence Public Schools

*

The Childrens' Summer Studio is an art school for children from
kindergarten through high-school age sponsored by the Recreation Council
of Lawrence, Kansas, a university town. This community of 27,000 people

is also a business center. An average of 200 children meet with about 7 teachers in half-day sessions for four weeks each summer to study drawing, painting, and crafts. The program has as its purposes to furnish constructive leisure activities for Lawrence children and to give teaching experience to art education majors in the University of Kansas.

All attendance is voluntary, and no fee is charged for any child enrolled in the Lawrence schools. Children at all levels of ability attend, both those with unusual talent and those struggling for self-expression. Teachers in the city schools often recommend to parents that gifted children attend the studio and as often advise slow learners to get help there.

The studio meets in a school building and is organized as a workshop. Kindergarten and first-grade children form a class in which a wide variety of activities takes place. All children from second grade through high school choose the shop in which they wish to work for the first half of the session. At the end of this time they may change to another class. The most popular classes are clay modeling, woodwork, painting, and design.

Teachers seek to stimulate children to do creative work based on personal experience. Exploration is encouraged, and many varied materials are provided with which to work. Regular activities include drawing, painting, clay modeling, woodcraft, weaving, leather-work, design, block printing, metal-work, carving, marionette and puppet craft, and paper craft. Relaxing periods feature poetry, songs, and reading.

When the program was originated, all financial support came from individuals and groups in the community. As a wider summer recreation program for Lawrence children grew, the studio became part of that program and was put under the direction of the Recreation Council and now draws its support from a fund in the community chest, as well as from the board of education.

* * *

DEPARTMENT OF ART EDUCATION PROGRAM FOR CHILDREN,
UNIVERSITY OF KANSAS, LAWRENCE, KANSAS

Maud Ellsworth, Associate Professor of Art Education

*

The department of art education of the University of Kansas sponsors a childrens' program of art education. This activity affords opportunity for growth in art expression to children of the Lawrence community and an opportunity for undergraduate and graduate students to do experimental work in art education and increase their skills in teaching.

Lawrence is a city of 23,000 inhabitants located 40 miles west of Kansas City in a farming community. It is an expanding business center and is experiencing a growth in new homes and industrial plants. It has a high school, a junior high school, and nine elementary schools.

The special art classes meet in art education rooms of the university, the childrens' activities room of the university art museum, and city schoolrooms. Seventy-five to 100 children from Grades I through XII of the city schools voluntarily attend each semester to engage in drawing, painting, clay modeling, woodcraft, weaving, block printing, metal-work, carving, puppet-work, and paper craft.

About a dozen student-teachers are active in the program each semester. These teachers have freedom to experiment with various educational methods. They consult with art education staff members and frequently hold discussion sessions with one another.

University credit is not given for working with these experimental groups. Teaching in the childrens' program is voluntary and is a part of the regular study of art education methods. Credit for student-teaching is earned off-campus in city school systems within a radius of 50 or 60 miles of Lawrence.

Classes are small (always less than 20) and are usually mixed-ability groups. The emphasis in all activities is to stimulate children to do creative work based on their own experience. Natural growth patterns and individual differences are taken into account, and search for personal ways of working is encouraged. Many different kinds of material are provided with which to work, and class activities are supplemented by field trips to see films and museum exhibits.

The city schools maintain art and music programs at all levels. Students in education do regular observation of teaching in the Lawrence schools, and many Lawrence teachers participate in workshops and other educational activities at the university. Lawrence teachers and administrators are particularly helpful in the university's program of art education for children. They co-operate in arranging for groups to attend classes, and they make recommendations to parents encouraging gifted children, children who need stimulation, or those with other needs, to come into the program.

* * *

BALTIMORE PUBLIC SCHOOLS, BALTIMORE 18, MARYLAND

John H. Fischer, Superintendent of Public Instruction

*

The Baltimore public schools are a system of 130 elementary, 24 junior high, 11 senior high, and 10 vocational and special units, serving about 150,000 students. These schools follow what is called a "normal progress program," whereby the great majority of pupils pass at the end of the year into the next higher grade, advancing in groups whose members are largely of about the same age and at the same stage of physical and emotional maturity. Within this general policy, provision is made for gifted students in the elementary schools by enrichment in the regular

classroom, some sectioned grades, some special-interest groups, and
limited acceleration. In the junior high schools enrichment is accompanied by segregation into classes for subjects in which students
show unusual interest and superior ability. There are two junior
high schools in which bright pupils may do the work of three years
in two years' time. Two demonstration schools, conducted in the
summer months, also provide acceleration by allowing intermediate-
grade pupils who attend them to advance about one-half year. In the
high schools special subject classes are provided for those with
unusual interest and ability. In addition, there are four high
schools in which advanced college-preparatory courses are offered,
permitting more capable students to save approximately a year in their
programs of posthigh-school education.

Identification of the gifted is based on information in a cumulative record that follows the student throughout his school program.
This record contains intelligence- and achievement-test data, grades,
information about special talents, guidance and conference notes, and
teachers' comments. Use of this information by teachers and guidance
personnel in each school results in the selection for special treatment of about 15 to 20 per cent of the student population.

As an example of enrichment on the elementary level, one school
has a school-wide activity day for the first two periods of every
Wednesday. Twelve groups run simultaneously: the pupil council,
visual-aids, music, art, science, dramatics, square-dancing, story-
telling, and some remedial-reading and arithmetic groups. Another
activity is carried on by the principal and vice-principal, who meet
once a week with 25 children selected by the teachers of Grades IV,
V, and VI. Twelve field trips are taken during the year by this group.
Two weeks are spent in preparation for a trip made in the third week.
Visits have been made to a school where a talented group demonstrated
puppet-making, to a school in a less economically privileged section
of the city, to a housing project, to historic and literary shrines,
museums, and libraries. Another special group, composed of exceptionally capable and socially mature third-graders, is offered enrichment
in science and music.

In addition to recommending certain students for enrichment activities, in special cases counselors may approve an elementary student
for a year's acceleration.

At the sixth-grade level, selected pupils and their parents are
made aware of the junior high school acceleration program. Recommendation for this program is made to the principal by the counselor after
a study of the pupil's record and consultation with him and his parents.
Approximately 3 per cent of junior high pupils are in this program.

In the eighth grade, accelerated curriculums are again brought to
the attention of pupils who would profit in the senior high school by
doing five years' work in four. About 5 per cent of high-school
students are enrolled in these curriculums. At the secondary level the
counselor also assists pupils in the choice of a course of study suited
to their abilities and interests, and special curricular activities are
brought to their attention. Able students are urged to participate in

preprofessional organizations, such as Future Teachers of America. These students are given the opportunity in some schools to assist teachers. Similar opportunities are afforded students interested in nursing to work in hospitals on a try-out basis.

Another area in which the students are aided by the counselsor is in the selection of a college. Assistance is offered in preparation for taking the College Board Examinations. Scholarships are brought to the attention of students who need this aid and help is given in applying for them.

By putting students in touch with community resources, such as the Maryland Institute, art museums, the Y Clubs, the Maryland Academy of Sciences, and Boy and Girl Scouts, an attempt is made to open up opportunities for pupils to use their talents outside school. Arrangements are often made to defray expenses in connection with these activities.

* * *

B. B. RUSSEL SCHOOL, BROCKTON, MASSACHUSETTS

Charles P. Reed, Principal

*

The Russel School is one of the elementary schools of Brockton, Massachusetts, an industrial community of 65,000 people. This school has 390 students and 14 faculty members. Two special enrichment classes for gifted children have been set up, one of 22 fourth- and fifth-graders and one of 23 fifth- and sixth-graders. The purpose of these classes is to develop maximum intellectual potentialities, leadership, creativity, and mental health.

Children are chosen for these special classes by means of group intelligence tests given in the third grade. Individual Binets are then administered to a select group, and further screening is made by the educational consultant and the child-guidance clinic staff.

A special feature of this program is its concern with mental health. The classes are designed to help the gifted avoid pitfalls in personality development. Casework and psychotherapy services are available whenever needed.

The curriculum for these special classes consists of arithmetic, spelling, language, social studies, reading science, literature, health, art, music, and physical education. These subjects are the same as those taught in the regular classes but are enriched. For example, the children may write an original play, make the costumes and scenery, and stage a show with puppets they have made or take the parts themselves.

Classroom activities are supplemented by field trips to museums, parks, and places of historic interest in Boston, Concord, Lexington, and Sudbury. Plymouth is visited at Thanksgiving time. Speakers and other programs from the community also come to the school.

* * *

WORCESTER ART MUSEUM, WORCESTER 2, MASSACHUSETTS

Minnie G. Levenson, Head, Division of Public Instruction

*

The Worcester Art Museum is located in Worcester, in central Massachusetts, a diversified industrial city of about 250,000 inhabitants. The museum offers, as a part of a larger program, professional instruction in art for children and youth of ages four through eighteen. The subjects taught are painting, drawing, block printing, and modeling with clay and other materials. The purpose of the activity is to provide all interested young people with early experience in the practice, understanding, and enjoyment of art. The average enrolment is about 1,250. The work with children is financed by the museum's private endowment, with additional support from the Cruikshank Fund.

The classes are free and open to all young people of the community and surrounding area, regardless of talent, and meet on two week days after school and on Saturday mornings. Groups are generally of the same age, but otherwise are heterogeneous. During the regular school term no two groups meet simultaneously, so that one teacher and her student assistants manage the program. During the summer the program is more extensive.

Children who are interested and have ability are encouraged to join the late-afternoon classes, which are less crowded than those on Saturday and offer more individual attention. A class in oil painting, for youths of fifteen to eighteen years, attracts those of more than ordinary ability. Such students are encouraged to enter the school of the Worcester Art Museum, where they can continue the study of art professionally.

Parents of the children are invited, once or twice a year, to view the work, meet the instructors, and discuss what the children are doing.

School-museum co-operation in Worcester is particularly close. The resources of the museum library--collections of slides, photographs, books, records, periodicals, and special school exhibits useful to the enrichment of many subject areas--are at the constant disposal of the teachers. The museum's staff is often called upon to assist in curriculum preparation. Gallery tours are a regular part of the sixth-grade art course of study in the Worcester schools. The museum also offers, in collaboration with Clark University, a teacher-training course which deals with methods of teaching, a study of mediums, curriculum, and sources for art in the school.

* * *

WORCESTER GIRLS' CLUB, WORCESTER 5, MASSACHUSETTS

Dora E. Dodge, Executive Director

*

The Worcester Girls' Club is a private organization located in this central Massachusetts industrial city of about 250,000 people. The club has as its purpose to train school-age girls of the community for responsible citizenship, especially as mothers of future citizens. To this end, the club presents a program designed to promote physical and mental health, to furnish training in all the home-making arts, and to stimulate interest in a wide range of cultural subjects. A small permanent staff is supplemented by many part-time and volunteer workers, who, altogether, serve several thousand girls in some way every year. Activities of the program include homecraft, handicraft, sewing, music, drama, dancing, gymnasium, swimming, and summer camp. The club has a small endowment but draws most of its support from the community chest.

The program is open to all Worcester girls of school age. The yearly dues are nominal.

The staff consists of an executive director, two house directors, one full-time leader in charge of each department, and part-time workers as needed. Although the program is not planned primarily for the gifted, the activities of some of the departments are of a kind that are stimulating to children with talent.

For example, in the music department 340 children, taught by 5 teachers, are in rhythm hand, piano, voice, and operetta work. Rhythm bands, for children of ages six through nine, teach basic rhythms by sight and sound and offer opportunity to become familiar with orchestral instruments. Groupwork is generally used in vocal and piano classes with beginners through the third grade in the music course, but some individual work is done with each child. Three recitals are given each year. Piano instruction for those six years old and over includes fundamentals, theory, rhythms, scales, arpeggios, and modern piano courses. Piano practice rooms are provided for those who have no other opportunity to use an instrument.

Voice instruction, for those eight years old and over, includes proper use of the voice, stage deportment, and development of a love for good music. Children study at their own pace.

Operetta classes, for ages nine through fourteen, are held once a week. Each spring an operetta is presented to the members of the club and public. Under the direction of specialists in drama, music, and the dance, the children from the regular classes of the club participate in the singing, dancing, and acting roles of the presentation.

* * *

JOHN BURROUGHS INTERMEDIATE SCHOOL, DETROIT 13, MICHIGAN

Frederick L. Schwass, Principal

*

Burroughs Intermediate School is a three-year junior high school of the Detroit school system, with an enrolment of about 1,270. The area immediately surrounding the school is a stable neighborhood of privately owned homes. Beyond the homes are groups of automotive and

related industrial plants. This school provides for about 160 of its
most gifted students by means of enrichment in homegeneous sections
within grades, enrichment in the regular classroom, and an arrangement for supplementary time for special activities at the end of the
school day. Approximately 15 teachers are engaged in this program.

At each promotion time, the elementary schools forward anecdotal
reports and records of all students that they are sending to Burroughs.
These reports and records contain such information as I.Q., achievement-
test scores, grades, and special abilities and are used to identify
gifted students.

Each grade has four to nine sections. Whenever possible, the
gifted students are placed in the upper section. Work is then provided
for each group appropriate to its ability. If the programing of homogeneous groups is not possible, the gifted are given special treatment
in their regular classes. This enrichment is offered in English,
auditorium, social studies, science, art, music, and practical arts.

For example, in social studies the superior students are encouraged to do supplementary reading, particularly of biographies, and to
report on new books in the library. Letters are exchanged with students
in foreign countries. Reports are made about historical radio and
television programs, and occasionally students have the opportunity to
appear on programs. Talented students also prepare such activities and
materials for the regular class program as biographical sketches,
readings for days of special historical interest, skits, maps, illustrated and annotated booklets, bulletin-board displays, and models of wood,
papier-mache, and plaster.

In mathematics classes, as another example, gifted students make
supplementary charts, maps, and drawings. Special assignments are given
on applications to business and industry, and models of various geometric
forms and designs are constructed. A mathematics club features recreation with number and figure puzzles. Special classes offer algebra to
those whose aptitude scores are high enough.

Supplementary time is made available in the morning before the
regular school periods and in a Seventh Hour Program afterward. Students with special talents and interests are offered various extra
activities. String and band instrument groups meet. Those interested
in poster and other art contests receive instruction. Shop students
put in additional time working with plastics and etching copper, brass,
and aluminum trays.

The glee clubs broadcast at least twice a year, and the gifted
instrumental pupils appear in concert with the All-City Orchestra and
Band. The band appears in a district concert once a year. The fine-
arts department presents a weekly program in the auditorium.

One evening of each fall an Open House Program is held for the
community. Gifted students play a large part in the choosing of a
theme and in the preparation for this event. Each department of the
school, often in co-operation with some community organization, prepares an exhibit or activity in keeping with the general theme,
usually one of national significance.

Community resources are used in a variety of ways. Gifted
science students visit the Detroit Zoo, Cranbrook Institute, and the
Edison Institute and power plants. Fine-arts students visit the art
museum, participate in Saturday morning classes held throughout the
city, and attend symphony concerts. A number of local, regional, and
national art and poster contests are entered. Practical-arts students
compete for Ford Industrial Arts Awards and participate in model air-
plane and boat-building contests. English students write short
stories and essays for the Scholastic Writing Awards Contest; enter
the Allied Youth competition, the American Legion competition, the
D.A.R. speech contest, the Detroit Times Oratorical Contest, and the
Detroit News Spelling Bee; and read poetry over a local radio station.

* * *

EDWIN DENBY HIGH SCHOOL, DETROIT 26, MICHIGAN

Irwin G. Wolf, Principal

*

Denby High School is one of the four-year secondary schools of the
Detroit public school system. It has an enrolment of 4,100 and a faculty of about 150. The community surrounding the school is largely one of
single, owner-occupied homes; the men of the community are mainly
craftsmen, foremen, operatives, and kindred workers. Special opportunities and experiences for gifted students in this school are provided,
for the most part, within the regular classroom, in art, music, English,
drama, radio broadcasting and script-writing, photography, and inter-
pretive dancing. There is a limited use of homogeneous classes. Special
extracurricular activities provide other opportunities, and several of
the clubs (Drama Club, Broadcasting Guild, Astronomy Club, Ad Club, Motion
Picture Discrimination Club, Science Club, and a Ham Operators' Group)
are particularly perinent to the interests and abilities of the gifted.

Superior students are identified by means of group intelligence
tests, aptitude and achievement tests, teachers' observations, and the
students' expression of interest. Concern is not limited to those who
rate high on intelligence tests. In all, about 20 per cent of the
student body receive special consideration in the program for gifted
and talented pupils.

Each semester one or two ninth-grade classes are designated as
Accelerated Reading Classes. Students admitted to these are of
eleventh-grade reading ability or better. Instead of reading from the
regular anthology, these pupils read such works as The Four Comedies
of Shakespeare, A Collection of Poetry, The House of the Seven Gables,
A Tale of Two Cities, and Kon Tiki. Vocabulary development takes place
in the context of the readings. Students are helped to see the historical and cultural settings of the stories by the use of pictures and
materials from the museum. Extensive outside reading of the classics
is encouraged. Through use of film strips, moving pictures, and class
discussion, the students are shown how story plots are developed.
Understanding of human-relations problems and other aspects of mature

novels are accomplished through panel and group discussions.

Another Accelerated Reading Class is offered to eleventh- and twelfth-graders who are readers of above average ability. This class, a six-week noncredit course, is taught by a faculty member who has also taught in college and is designed to help potential college Freshment accomplish the heavy reading schedule of their first year.

The radio and speech classes and the Broadcasting Guilds are other examples of the Denby program. These groups are composed of all students who have an interest in radio and television, but the more talented ones are usually elected to, or assume, key positions in the activities. An orientation period of several weeks is followed by about fourteen weeks of workshop activities. These consist of six radio productions written and produced by the classes. In addition to the regular productions, a five-minute newscast is given at the beginning of each class period. Students write, time, and read their own news. A class critique is written for each program. In this way the better programs and the more talented students are selected to appear on the radio station owned and operated by the Detroit schools. Superior students also study propaganda techniques and give illustrated reports to the class during the weekly evaluation of network commentators and newscasters. More advanced work is done by the Broadcasting Guilds on an extracurricular basis before and after school. Students interested in electronics are engaged in designing a radio studio to be equipped with turntables, mixers, and recorders. The guilds make twice daily broadcasts of school announcements over the public address system. They write and produce assembly programs for the entire school and do special programs for individual classes. Poetry is recorded for use in English classes. Language recordings are made. Continuity is written for music department broadcasts. Publicity is prepared for plays and other school activities. Announcers are provided for assemblies, meets, and games. Many speeches are made each year in the day and evening schools on behalf of the Red Cross blood bank.

Community resources are used by the school program in a number of ways. Business and industry offer supervised experiences for talented students. The Economic Club of Detroit provides transportation for student field trips to places of business, factories, and stores. During the summer, the recreation department offers opportunities for young people to perform service activities. Local radio stations occasionally use talented students on both public service and commercial programs. The Detroit Institute of Art Museum offers Saturday morning art classes which are attended by gifted Enby students.

* * *

UNIVERSITY CITY PUBLIC SCHOOLS, UNIVERSITY CITY 5, MISSOURI

Julius E. Warren, Superintendent

*

The University City public schools are a system of 8 elementary, 1 primary, 2 junior high, and 1 senior high schools with a combined enrolment of about 7,500. University City is a residential, upper-middle-class community of average wealth. The population, presently about 50,000, is growing rapidly. Gifted elementary-school pupils are provided for in special enrichment classes that meet twice each week during school time in each of the schools of the city. About 10 per cent of the enrolment in Grades III, IV, V, and VI participate in these classes. In junior high schools, pupils who have participated in the enrichment program at the elementary-school level and other superior pupils ranking in the upper 2 or 3 per cent are grouped together in four of the fourteen or fifteen sections of Grades VII, VIII, and IX. Altogether, about 25 per cent of the junior high school enrolment are in these special sections. Numerous clubs, athletics, drama, and music activities offer enrichment to students, at both the junior and the senior high school levels.

Candidates for enrichment classes may be referred by their teachers for consideration or may be selected as a result of the regular review of the permanent records of all students. These records include one or more group intelligence-test and achievement-test scores which are used to screen promising candidates. An individual test is administered to all children who appear likely to benefit from enrichment. The classroom teacher then fills out a form describing the specific strengths and weaknesses of each candidate. The child's entire record is next reviewed by the enrichment class teacher, the principal, and the school psychologist. Final selection of candidates is based on classwork, school marks, and general performance as shown by the permanent record and special techniques used in screening. Those chosen represent the top 1 per cent of school children in general, with I.Q.'s of 140 and above.

The size of the enrichment group varies from school to school and from grade to grade, depending upon the number of children who seem to need this type of program. The maximum number is generally 10. Whenever possible, only children from a single grade are grouped together. Three or more groups are organized at each school, depending on the need.

These groups meet with their special teacher for 40 or 50 minutes twice a week. The enrichment work may take several forms. It may be a development of the work of the regular classroom (particularly in social studies or science), a project of benefit to a grade (such as the preparation of a bibliography), an activity of benefit to the whole school (such as an assembly program), or a study of particular interest and benefit to the special students themselves.

Projects generally center on specific study areas or themes, such as communications, housing, or health. Activities in art, creative writing, music, drama, and the like are usually involved in the development of the projects. Reading, discussion, and written and oral reporting are supplemented by trips to make firsthand observations, by construction of models or equipment, and by preparation of charts, graphs, maps, and pictorial representations which the children need to enhance their projects.

These enrichment classes are provided as an integral part of the regular school program, like speech classes, band and orchestra instruction, remedial-reading classes, office-helpers groups, and other

similar extra-class activities. No special publicity is given to them,
and they are treated like any other provision to meet individual needs.

* * *

THE FIELDSTON SCHOOL, FIELDSTON ROAD, NEW YORK 71, NEW YORK
Luther H. Tate, Principal

*

The Fieldston School is a private academic secondary school, one
of the Ethical Culture schools in New York City. It has an enrolment
of 575, and a staff of 52 full-time and 10 part-time faculty. In the
program of this school some devices which act to promote the interests
of outstanding students are provided, such as special classes and
affiliation with the School and College Study of Admission with Advanced Standing. However, effort is made to serve the gifted primarily
by motivating them through the total attitude held toward education
and not by special devices.

Fieldston tries to promote the idea that it is a pleasure to do
things well and that becoming educated is an interesting process. The
process of education is emphasized, not the rewards. The school is
restrained in its use of marks as a prod to better work. The aspects
of teaching that deal with making judgments of performance are mini-
mized, and emphasis is placed on aspects of sharing experience between
teachers and pupils.

Where it is practical and considered desirable, the school tries
to make provision for the special interests and aptitudes of all
students. Accordingly, certain measures are taken that act to the
advantage of the gifted. For example, mathematics sections are
programed simultaneously and are homogeneous as to ability in mathematics. Selection for each section is made in department conferences
and is based on grades, standardized-test scores, and the judgment of
teachers. There is movement between sections during the year, as more
accurate judgments or changes in individuals warrant. A similar
program is in operation in the language department.

In certain other subjects, particularly the sciences, students
may elect the maximum or minimum course. Differences lie largely in
the laboratory work or the extent of the mathematical applications of
the fundamental concepts. Examinations include some questions for the
maximum students only.

In its participation in the School and College Study of Admission
with Advanced Standing, Fieldston deviates from the practice of some of
the other schools in the study by expecting that the students themselves will do nearly all the work of preparation. Teachers help by
assigning units of study and by clearing up difficulties which are
encountered, but there is a minimum of recitation and a minimum of
anticipation of difficulties by the teachers.

* * *

* * *

HUNTER COLLEGE ELEMENTARY SCHOOL, NEW YORK 21, NEW YORK
Florence N. Brumbaugh, Principal

*

Hunter College Elementary School is a public nursery, kinder-garten, and six-year elementary school connected with Hunter College in New York City. It has an enrolment of 450 pupils and a faculty of 23. It is an experimental laboratory school for the education of gifted children and the training of teachers of the gifted. The emphasis in the curriculum is on enrichment, provided both in the regular classroom subjects and in the special activities.

Each year 50 to 75 pupils are admitted to replace the numbers who leave to enter the various junior high schools. Students are drawn from all economic classes. The Binet test is given each ap-plicant, and a minimum score of 130 is required. Achievement-test scores must be commensurate with the average of those students of the same age and sex according to I.Q. Admission is then made from the top of the list down for as many individuals of each age as there are places to fill. Each child visits the school for a half-day to enable the teacher to appraise his social and emotional maturity, while one or both parents are interviewed by the admissions committee.

The school has set up a number of goals for the curriculum, in-cluding sound mental and physical health, learning to become econom-ically competent, developing skills in social relationships, understanding the role of world citizenship. The entire school program is planned to promote good mental hygiene through the life of the school. Problems that are too complex for teachers to handle are referred to specialists, in some cases the college educational clinic or faculty members who specialize in child-guidance and behavior problems. Considerable use is made of objective tests for measuring achievement and personal traits as a means of diagnosing problem cases. The record-keeping system is more comprehensive than that in most schools. Reporting to parents is done chiefly through individual conferences, though written reports are also used to inform them of pupil progress in terms of school objectives.

Class groups are based on chronological age and range in size from 15 to 20 pupils in the nursery to from 25 to 28 in the higher-age groups. There is an attempt to keep the number of boys and girls equal in each class. At each level there are two or three classes of the same age. Individuals are placed in one of these groups primarily on the basis of social and emotional need and may be transferred to another at any time.

The school follows the Course of Study for New York Schools as a minimum. Enrichment beyond this is planned by the Hunter staff and takes many forms. Responsibility for class procedure rests largely with the classroom teacher. Life in the classroom tends to be informal, with a workshop atmosphere prevailing, but self-discipline and respon-sibility are stressed. Much learning is achieved through direct experiencing. Emphasis is on the unified approach to subject matter, capitalizing relatedness in developing basic themes for study. Enrichment is achieved mainly through the use of a wide array of instructional resources. Occasionally, certain pupils are accelerated.

The three R's, the social studies, science, health, literature, the arts and crafts, and physical education, all have a place in the school curriculum. Considerable attention is paid to the academic skills that are required for success in both school work and daily living, such as oral and written language, reading, spelling, and penmanship. As far as possible, these skills are treated as tools for problem-solving in various curriculum areas. Music, arts and crafts, foreign languages, and physical education are taught by special teachers who are experts in these areas, and the instruction is related to other class projects.

An important feature of school life at Hunter is the club period. For one hour each week other school activities cease, and interest groups meet for activities in art, cooking, dancing, dramatics, French, poetry, photography, radio workshop, science, hobbies (stamps and coins), and music. Pupils try out for the clubs, since each group is limited to fifteen members without reference to age. Sponsoring teachers make the final decision in terms of interest and ability shown. A child may, if he prefers, engage in an individual hobby during this period. Many of the activities of the clubs are carried on at other times in the classroom, and those in the clubs share experiences with their classmates who would enjoy them equally but belong to other groups. Sometimes club activities are described or demonstrated to the entire school at assemblies.

Educational activities at the school frequently range beyond the classrooms, as teachers and students take advantage of the cultural resources of New York City and its surroundings. Many visits are made to the shops of the immediate neighborhood, the museums, historic monuments, United Nations' headquarters, industrial plants, exhibits, parks, libraries, and the foreign settlements of the city. Groups and individuals now and then appear on radio and television programs. Occasional camping trips are made.

Enterprises are undertaken each year in which the children perform public services. Aid is given to needy childrens' groups, entertainment programs are put on, and community benefit campaigns, such as the Christmas Seal and Red Cross drives and the March of Dimes, receive cooperation. The students play a major role in the planning and carrying-out of their part in these activities.

* * *

SEWANHAKA HIGH SCHOOL, FLORAL PARK, NEW YORK

Harold W. Wright, Supervising Principal

*

Sewanhaka High School is a four-year comprehensive central high school with an enrolment of about 4,500 and a faculty of 250. The school serves four Union Free school districts, embracing four incorpor-

ated and several unincorporated villages. The community is located on
Long Island just outside the New York City limits and is mostly residential, with some sprinkling of light industry. The program offered
to about 500 of its most gifted students is one of general enrichment
in the regular classroom for Grades IX through XII, a special seminar
for Seniors, and some honor classes in social studies and English.

Each year Freshment with superior scholastic aptitudes are included in this general program. The selection is revised in the Sophomore
year on the basis of teachers' observations, achievement, improvement
in reading, and the results of any further testing.

The principal assigns a committee of fifteen teachers to work
with the guidance director in counseling and directing the education
of the students in the program. This committee also may assist and
advise classroom teachers. The committee chairman is a member of the
Metropolitan School Study Council Committee for exceptional children.

The activities in social studies are an example of enrichment
for the gifted in the regular classroom. Procedures may include
appointing committees with gifted pupils as chairmen, giving assignments requiring library research, using study guides with optional
critical-thought questions, and frequent use of class discussion.
Several honors classes in social studies are open to superior students.

Pupils are admitted to honors classes in English on the basis of
interest and ability. Enrichment procedures in these classes include
special training in the development of more mature composition work,
granting of considerable freedom for pupils in choosing research
projects, and extensive supplementary reading program, discussion of
literature on a comparative basis, and incorporation into the course
of background material from English and American literature, art, and
music.

Students for the Senior seminar group are chosen at the end of the
Junior year. Selection is made on the basis of past scholastic achievement and scholastic aptitude (better than a 90 average and an I.Q. above
130, or better than a 95 average and an I.Q. above 125), results of the
Ohio Psychological Test, recommendations by teachers and administrative
personnel, membership in the Honor Society, interview with each recommended student by members of the current seminar and the co-ordinator,
and parental approval. The final choice of not more than 25 students
is made by the co-ordinator after all information has been assembled.

The seminar group meets once a week. Each member selects and
plans a learning activity related to one or more of his regular subjects.
Special privileges are granted these students for use of in- and out-
of-school facilities, so that many resources can be used. In seminar
meetings students discuss their activity study and exchange information
and views. They also invite specialists in the school, such as the head
of the English department, the psychologist, the psychiatrist, a
chemistry teacher, or an art teacher, to meet with them for discussion.
Field trips to theaters, courthouses, museums, exhibits, and concert
halls round out the seminar activities.

* * *

* * *

NEW YORK CITY SCHOOLS, BROOKLYN 1, NEW YORK
William Jansen, Superintendent of Schools

*

The New York City schools comprise a group of some 600 elementary,
300 junior high, and 70 senior high schools. Provision for gifted students is made at all levels of the system. In about 19 elementary
schools special classes for intellectually gifted children offer enrichment within the regular school program. Some 62 regular junior
high schools provide special progress classes that allow superior
students to complete three years' work in two years' time. Enrichment
classes are also offered for those gifted students not wishing an
accelerated program. On the high-school level qualified students may
enrol in honors classes, honors schools, or specialized high schools.
Honors classes are found in most of the 54 academic high schools.
Eight of the academic high schools have organized schools for the
gifted within their regular organizations. Of the 16 high schools
offering special work in various fields, 4 center about purposes that
tend to select students of superior ability.

* * *

JUNIOR HIGH SCHOOL DIVISION, NEW YORK CITY SCHOOLS,
BROOKLYN 1, NEW YORK
Mary A. Kennedy, Assistant Superintendent in Charge of Curriculum

*

The Junior High School Division of the New York City schools includes about 110 schools offering work in the seventh, eighth, and ninth
grades. The program planned for gifted pupils in these schools is an
integral part of the general education program for junior high school
pupils. Those who meet the prescribed requirements may apply, upon
completing the sixth grade, for admission to special progress classes
which provide enrichment and acceleration. These classes are distributed
throughout the four boroughs in 62 schools. Altogether, about 10,000
students are taught in 300 classes by 1,500 teachers. Should parents of
gifted children not wish them to have an accelerated program, other
provision is made through a program of enrichment. In some schools
special classes are also offered for the artistically gifted.

To be admitted to the special progress class program, a promoted
sixth-year student must have an I.Q. of at least 130, have a reading
grade placement of 8.5, have an arithmetic grade placement of 8.0, be at
least eleven years old, have a record of superior school achievement,
and be physically fit and emotionally stable.

The special progress classes are so named because pupils in them
complete three years of schooling in two years' time. The seventh grade

and half of the eighth are completed during the first year, and the
second half of the eighth grade and all of the ninth are covered in
the second year. Graduates of these classes enter the tenth grade of
senior high school.

Leadership training is an important phase of special progress instruction. Higher standards of scholarship are expected of the pupils,
and emphasis is placed on originality of work and the use of research
techniques. It is also desired that the children in these classes
develop a sensitivity to social problems which will permit the fullest
understanding of the democratic system.

To achieve these goals, the regular curriculum of Grades VII,
VIII, and IX is followed, but in a way adapted to the needs and abilities
of gifted pupils. For example, in the language-arts courses extensive
reading is encouraged in current and classical literature, including
modern and traditional historical novels. This reading program aims at
providing the special progress pupil with intermediate and advanced
reading skills which will help make him a discriminating and efficient
reader.

Special accent is placed on creative writing. Pupils are encouraged to write scripts for presentation over the public address system
and for inclusion in school newspapers and magazines. Often these works
are broadened into full-length playlets or novelettes. Students are
given opportunity to engage in research. Some compile anthologies of
poetry and prose. Panel discussions, mock trials, and public forums
also constitute a generous share of the program. Students take an
active part in the preparation of presentations for assemblies and
parents' meetings.

The total curriculum for special progress classes includes English,
social studies, mathematics, science, foreign language, health education,
industrial arts, library, fine arts, and music. Special progress
pupils are programed to work with pupils of the regular classes in
gymnasium, clubwork, assemblies, the student council and other similar
activities, and certain special art and music classes.

After the pupil personnel of the special progress classes have
been selected, very often there remains a group that has not quite
measured up to the requirements of eligibility. These students, together
with some who, though eligible, do not enter the special progress classes
because of parents' wishes, constitute the membership of the enrichment
classes.

In addition to providing special classes for intellectually gifted
children, the junior high schools offer special opportunities and
training for children with talents in music, art, and dancing. Frequently
these children are identified in the sixth year of the feeder schools,
so that their training may begin early in the seventh year. Individual
programs are provided for the particular needs of each pupil, whenever
possible. In many cases the children have extra periods assigned in their
areas of talent. After-school instruction and practice are frequently
made available. Auditorium exercises, in-school and out-of-school
broadcasting, art exhibitions, talent shows, operettas, and recitals
offer other opportunities for talented artists to exercise and develop
their talents.

Gifted pupils under teacher guidance often survey the community to gather news and report to their classes regarding new developments in settlement houses, parks, churches, and the like. Under teacher guidance they also assist in scheduling visits for agents of the government, speakers from the police and fire departments and welfare agencies. When the schools co-operate with neighborhood agencies in cleanup campaigns and safety drives, gifted students also take the lead.

* * *

NEW YORK CITY ACADEMIC HIGH SCHOOLS, BROOKLYN 2, NEW YORK

C. Frederick Pertsch, Associate Superintendent in
Charge of High Schools

*

The New York City academic high schools are a group of 54 four-year high schools attended by some 159,000 students. These schools are scattered throughout the five boroughs of the city. Their programs have common elements; yet, serving different socio-economic areas, they have developed programs to fit varied needs. This is true of their programs for the gifted. In general, however, there are three types of organization that care for the needs of the gifted: four separate specialized schools, honor schools within schools, and honor classes.

Methods used to identify the gifted students vary. Fifty-one schools use I.Q. as an identification factor, the minimum qualifying score varying from 110 to 130. Most schools use I.Q. in conjunction with teachers' recommendations and students' grades. Of the four special high schools, two--the Bronx High School of Science and Stuyvesant High School--have competitive entrance examinations. Brooklyn Technical High School has an entrance examination but also considers elementary-school scholastic record and the recommendation of the elementary-school principal. The High School of Music and Art bases its selection upon aptitude in creative art or music.

Stuyvesant and the Bronx High School of Science offer a specialized program of science and mathematics for college-bound pupils. Brooklyn Technical offers a similar program, as well as a technological course for gifted pupils who do not intend to go to college. The High School of Music and Art gives a college-preparatory course with special emphasis on creative art and music.

Eight academic high schools have organized separate schools for the gifted within their regular school organizations. In this type of school, gifted pupils are segregated in practically all classes except health education, study hall, and lunch.

There are special classes in 42 of the schools for pupils of superior attainment in particular subjects. The members of these classes follow an enriched course in the subject for which they show special aptitude, while attending regular classes in other subjects.

In addition to these provisions, the size of the schools in New York City permits varied curriculum offerings in special fields, such as art, music, poetry, drama, script-writing, advanced science, and advanced mathematics. Numerous other means are also employed by the schools to help the gifted and develop initiative and leadership, such as school government, clubs, forums, assemblies, school and specialized department publications, and social functions.

An extensive use of community resources is made by the schools in their programs for the gifted. For example, the museums of the city circulate exhibits among the schools. Special science, art, and music programs are arranged in conjunction with community organizations. Industrial institutes, social studies forums, ballet, opera, and drama are frequently attended. Systematic help is given to those interested in the Westinghouse Science Talent Search. Students are also given assistance in obtaining the awards offered by other industrial and professional organizations of the community.

* * *

PUBLIC SCHOOL NO. 241, NEW YORK CITY DIVISION OF ELEMENTARY SCHOOLS, BROOKLYN 25, NEW YORK

Frieda R. Shprentz, Principal

*

Public School No. 241, Brooklyn, is one of the 600 elementary schools of New York City. It has an enrolment of 1,382 and a faculty of 48 and is located in a prosperous middle-class community with cultural advantages. Many of the parents are professional people. This school is one of the some 19 elementary schools of the city that are officially credited with operating a special program for their intellectually gifted children. These programs provide enrichment in special classes for gifted children without isolating them from the total school program. In P.S. 241, 7 full- and part-time teachers conduct four special classes serving 129 children.

In the third grade, pupils are given city-wide intelligence, reading, and arithmetic tests. The children with I.Q.'s of 130 or higher and reading grade placements of 5 or higher are considered for the fourth-grade special class. At a supervisor-teacher conference these students are discussed, and a final decision is made on the basis of social maturity, emotional stability, leadership potential, achievement, and I.Q. When the children have completed the sixth grade, they are eligible, upon recommendation of their teachers, for a special seventh-grade class in a junior high school. Some do not elect to attend the junior high school, and at P.S. 241 facilities are provided for this group to work together in a seventh-grade class.

The special classes in the fourth, fifth, and sixth grades offer work in language arts, mathematics, science, social studies, art, crafts, ceramics, music, health, and other areas. All subjects are taught by the class teacher, supplemented by specialists in ceramics and music. The seventh-grade group works on a departmental system, though their homeroom teacher is assigned to them for language arts, social studies, and library work. Enrichment in this group is provided in every subject area. Children in all the special groups attend regular school assemblies and participate in all school activities.

Creative expression by both the individual child and the group is encouraged and practiced by means of activities in ceramics, painting, sculpture, wood-carving, and other handwork. The school makes extensive use of the educational opportunities provided by near-by museums, botanic gardens, libraries, and parks.

As for language-arts activities, the writing of original prose and verse is an essential component of all areas of learning in P.S. 241. In addition to original booklets, the children write and direct their own plays, puppet shows, and operettas for class, school, and community presentation. The children also produce a school magazine in which their creative writing is published. The principal and teachers, as well as students, bring in books to share with the others. The school library provides reading materials for their particular interests. Each special class has a set of encyclopedias and other reference materials in the room.

Continuous provision is made for assisting children in developing maximum resourcefulness and social competency. Children are encouraged to contribute to class and school planning. A school science center with a student consulting service was planned and executed by a sixth-year special class. These children collected, constructed, and prepared materials which other children in the school are now using. Children in the special classes share their knowledge and experiences with other children of the school. Frequently they give talks to other classes, sometimes illustrated by slides that they have made. They portray historical characters and events through their plays, poems, songs, and assembly programs.

All classroom activities provide opportunities for practice in democratic living. Additional opportunities are provided through the election of class officers and representatives to the school youth council and through the representation of the school in a community council. Children in these classes also assume leadership in school government and in special activities, such as participation in the community bazaar, caring for the school audio-visual program, distributing milk, arranging for school dances, and participating in athletic activities.

* * *

BRONX HIGH SCHOOL OF SCIENCE, NEW YORK 68, NEW YORK

Morris Meister, Principal

*

The Bronx High School of Science is one of the four specialized academic high schools in the High School Division of the New York City schools. As a specialized school it is nonzoned and admits qualified students who live anywhere within the city boundaries. All socio-

economic levels are represented in the student body of 2,400; but, for
the most part, students come from middle-class homes. The faculty of
126 is recruited from a city-wide pool of teachers licensed by a board
of examiners. The entire curriculum of the school is designed for the
gifted and includes the range of subjects usually offered in an
academic high school. However, the particular purpose of the program
is to give able boys and girls with special interests in mathematics
and science an opportunity to explore and develop those interests.
The enriched program is supplemented by advanced elective courses in
science and mathematics and by provisions for acceleration under the
Early Admission to College and the Admission to College with Advanced
Standing programs.

The school admits its students by a selective process. All candidates are required to take a written admissions test covering verbal
ability, mathematics skill, and arithmetic reasoning ability. The
applicant's school record must also be approved, a satisfactory
recommendation obtained from the guidance counselor, and parents'
consent must be given. For some of the applicants an interview
designed to ascertain the genuineness of the student's interest in
science and mathematics is also a part of the admission procedure.
About one-third to one-fourth of the applicants are admitted.

Guidance for the students is the special responsibility of the
Guidance Committee of twelve teachers. At least three personal
interviews are held with each student, for orientation, for discussion
of elective choices, and for an evaluation of his record and advice
about college jobs. Group guidance in these same areas is given more
extensively through the homeroom program. Other group meetings provide
social, vocational, and college guidance (including how to obtain
scholarships) and are usually addressed by a guest resource person.
For emotionally disturbed students a social worker is made available
through funds supplied by the parents' association.

The first year of the school offers an integrated program of
English, social studies, science, and mathematics. The Sophomore and
Junior years emphasize general educational values and aim to prepare
students to meet the admission requirements of both liberal arts
colleges and engineering and technical schools. Students then pursue
any special interests that they may have developed within the sciences
and mathematics in their earlier years of work.

In the biological sciences a basic course is offered, with a year
in clinical laboratory techniques. Or a field biology course can be
chosen, in which there is opportunity to study plant and animal life and
geological features in the parks surrounding New York City. In the
physical sciences, basic courses in physics, chemistry, industrial
arts, and mechanical drawing are supplemented by numerous electives on
elementary and advanced levels.

Each science course is liberally provided with laboratory work.
The completely equipped laboratories of the school provide every
facility for various types of individual and group projects and make
possible experiments connected with both classwork and hobbies.

In mathematics a four-year sequence is available including courses
in algebra, geometry, intermediate algebra, trigonometry, and solid

geometry. Advanced courses are offered in higher geometry, algebra, and calculus. In addition to his science specialties, each student takes four years of English and four years of social studies, three years of a foreign language, a four-year program of health education, as well as art and music appreciation. These are frequently integrated with one another and with the sciences. In addition, a course called "Techniques of Public Discussion" is organized for students concerned with improving their ability to take part in group discussions, either as leaders or as participants.

Classwork is enriched by means of several procedures. Students do extensive outside reading, make reports, and occasionally teach a class. Participation is encouraged and guidance provided in the preparation for mathematics and science exhibitions and competitions, such as the Science Fair, the Westinghouse Talent Search, and the Interscholastic Mathematics League competition. A large number of school clubs concentrate their interests in science activities related to the school courses, as well as numerous activities of generalized interest. A full program of varsity and intramural sports is developed under the guidance of the Student Organization. The Student Organization is also in charge of a students' store, which conducts a $50,000-a-year business. Membership in the Student Organization entitles students to a purchase card with which many items of school supplies can be purchased at practically wholesale prices. The store itself is on a nonprofit basis, and the savings for those who patronize the store usually cover the cost of membership dues in the Student Organization.

The parents' group of the school makes available a number of community resources. Among these are speakers, career-guidance panels, special excursions to places of educational and scientific interest, and many social and recreational activities. In addition, the parents arrange for a lecture series and other activities in which a great many of the faculty participate, such as the week-end biology camp financed by the parents and conducted by members of the faculty.

The school also uses various other community resources in its program, by means of visits to municipal hospitals, college research laboratories, the American Museum of Natural History, the New York Botanical Gardens, the Zoological Gardens, and the Museum of the City of New York.

* * *

BROOKLYN TECHNICAL HIGH SCHOOL, BROOKLYN 17, NEW YORK

William Pabst, Principal

*

Brooklyn Technical High School is one of the four special high schools in the New York City high-school system which center about purposes that tend to attract students of a high level of ability. It has a daytime enrolment of approximately 5,700 and a teaching staff of

280. This school offers both a technical and a general education in four years. It prepares students for immediate entry into industry, as well as for engineering college.

Any student living within the city limits may apply for entrance to Brooklyn Technical. Admission is on a competitive basis and is determined by a rating based on school record and degree of recommendation by the previous principal, I.Q., special aptitude for mathematics, and score on the entrance tests.

The first two years of each course are the same and consist of mathematics, science, drawing, and shop. This work is exploratory and foundational and is designed to give the training and experience necessary to make a choice of course for the last two years.

Several other types of guidance are offered by the school program. Each term the chairman of the various courses of study, together with the teachers in their departments, meet with interested students to explain what the several departments have to offer and what opportunities are open to graduates. Practicing engineers, chemists, industrial designers, and architects are invited to these conferences. Each student has a group adviser, who is always available to him for conferences. Many of the teachers are graduate engineers with many years of practical experience and are qualified to give advice. The school library contains many books on careers. A placement bureau assists both students and graduates. Extensive information is also supplied students about engineering and other colleges, their entrance requirements, programs of study, and scholarships offered.

The differentiated technical courses of the third and fourth years are designed to limit selection to a few broad fields of training. Study is offered in the fields of aeronautics, architecture, industrial arts, chemistry, electricity, mechanics, structure, and industrial design.

In addition to the technical courses, the school also offers a preparatory course for direct admission to higher technical schools. The required subjects in this course are English, mathematics, American history, economics, foreign language, technical drawing, shopwork, hygiene, and health education.

Academic subjects are taught by teachers with the same qualifications as those required in any academic high school, although their teaching conforms to the special needs of the technical program and the technically minded pupils. Teachers of special technical subjects must have degrees in engineering and to have had experience identical to that required of teachers in trade or industrial high schools.

The school building, with its shops, laboratories, drawing rooms, and other facilities, plays a considerable part in the enrichment of the program. Among the forty shops are pattern, foundry, sheet-metal, machine, engine, aeronautical, electrical construction, structural steel, and building constructions shops. In addition to the regular chemistry and physics laboratories, there are those specially equipped for studying strength of materials, power (steam, gas, air, and water), advanced chemistry, industrial chemistry, and metallurgy.

While station WNYE serves all the schools of New York City, its technical operation and production activities are carried on largely by the staff of Brooklyn Technical High School. Instruction is given to students in script-writing, radio production, radio speech, broadcasting operation, and sound recording. There is a special course in broadcast-station operation for a select group of Senior electrical students. The final examination for this course consists of appearing before the federal radio inspector to take an examination for the license of first-class broadcast-station operator.

* * *

FOREST HILLS HIGH SCHOOL, NEW YORK CITY

Dr. Leo R. Ryan, Principal

*

Forest Hills is a general four-year high school in a suburban community of greater New York City. The area was formerly entirely a residential one but now includes many apartment houses. Residents vary in income from very low to very high. The school has an enrolment of 3,300 and a faculty of 150. The program it provides its most gifted students covers, at present, the areas of science, mathematics, English, and social studies and involves about 24 teachers, directly and indirectly, and some 160 students. This program features special honors classes and offers an enriched and advanced curriculum.

The science and mathematics programs are particularly well developed. In the ninth-grade general science course, students are given a complete description of the special program and are offered an opportunity to participate in some of its activities. About 40 students who want to make science a four-year major or their lifework, apply and, with their parents' consent, are accepted. There are no rigid intelligence requirements for entrance into the program, but students who are successful in it usually have an I.Q. of 130 or above, reading and arithmetic placement scores well beyond the ninth grade, a scholastic average of above 90, placement in the ninetieth percentile or above on the Science Research Associates Test of Primary Abilities, and a score of 4 on the Man-to-Man Rating Scale used by the school.

Those choosing this program enter upon three years of honors work in biology, physics, chemistry, and mathematics. In addition, each student takes social studies and one language for the full four years of high school. The honors are taught by special teachers. Both subject teachers and the department chairman act as advisers. The chairman maintains continuity of guidance by assigning a sponsor to each student for the duration of his school career.

In their science classes these students are offered an opportunity to engage in research, learn laboratory techniques and the use of laboratory equipment, and gain skills in shopwork. Library research is also a part of each course, and required reading includes college

tests in biology, physics, and chemistry. Training in mathematics
includes a special class that goes as far as calculus. Recently a
course in college physics was organized by a group of students.

Students prepare exhibits of their work for demonstration
before other students or at the Science Fair sponsored by the Feder-
ation of Science Teacher Associations of New York. Reports of
student work are prepared for the school science journal or may be
presented at the seminar meetings of the school Science Society or
Mathematics Honor Society. Those who offer the best reports in
biology are invited to submit their work at a Biology Congress
sponsored by the New York Association of Biology Teachers. Students
also participate in the Westinghouse Science Talent Search.

After a half-year in the honors program, students who wish are
given the opportunity to enter an advanced science class. This is
a laboratory period in which the student selects his own research
problem and solves it, with a minimum of assistance from teachers.

Aside from their daily schedule of one period of science, one
period of mathematics, and possibly one period of laboratory work
on a personal project, students in the honors program participate
in the regular classes and activities of the school.

Where opportunities warrant, five or six of the best students
are placed in industrial, college, and research laboratories to
assist scientists at work. Many field trips are also made to such
places as the Edison, Sloan-Kettering, and the Brookhaven atomic
experimental laboratories, as well as to the zoos and museums of
New York.

In the social studies, gifted students are selected in the ninth
year and placed in honors classes in modern and American history. In
addition, these students have an opportunity to take a course in which
they are taught discussion techniques as they investigate current
problems of democracy. These students help conduct city-wide forums
with representatives of other schools.

In English, gifted students are selected and are given not only
honors courses in English but courses in journalism and dramatics.
During their "free" periods these students write for or edit the
school paper and the school magazine, conduct a column in the "town"
paper, the Queens Post, or are involved in the dramatics program.

In September, 1955, an advanced school is to begin operation.
Under this program selected students will be offered classes in social
studies, English, science, and mathematics, ending in college-type
work. Those students completing these courses will be able to apply
for advanced standing in college.

*   *   *

* * *

HIGH SCHOOL OF MUSIC AND ART, NEW YORK 31, NEW YORK

Edwin A. Kane, Acting Principal

*

The High School of Music and Art is one of the specialized academic high schools of the city of New York. It has a staff of 99 and an enrolment of 1,860. Its program provides for those who are highly talented and are planning to become professionals and for those who, as amateurs, may become community leaders in the fields of music and art. For each student, music or art is a chief subject of interest, in addition to regular academic studies--English, foreign languages, social studies, mathematics, and sciences.

Students from all parts of the city apply during their eighth or ninth year for admission as first-ninth-year or second-tenth-year students, respectively. Entrance examinations are designed to test for native capacity, not for acquired techniques. Thus the student body represents every element of the community and the widest range of social and economic levels within it. Application forms are distributed annually to the elementary, the junior high, and the parochial schools. Each applicant receives an individual appointment for the entrance examination in music or art. Of the 2,000 or more candidates who take the examination, some 500 (half in art, half in music) are accepted for admission.

In music, candidates are tested for sense of pitch, sense of rhythm, tonal memory, and harmonic sensitivity. Individual reactions to these tests are recorded. Those who sing or play an instrument are judged for tonal quality, co-ordination of hands and muscles, response to musical suggestion, and natural taste and interpretation.

In art, each candidate is required to submit a portfolio, but the work done in the presence of the examining teachers receives greater emphasis as a basis for judgment. Reactions to lines, to forms, and to colors are particularly noted. The co-ordination of hand and eye is observed. Evidence of imagination and originality of approach is noted, and visual memory is tested.

The regular academic program of five major subjects and three periods of music or art makes the daily schedule of the students at Music and Art a heavy one in terms of time and energy. For this reason some of the customary extracurricular activities have been incorporated into the work of regular classes. For example, one English class made up of select students is virtually a dramatics society, which produces plays for the school. Another class is the editorial board of the annual yearbook. Similar special activities are handled this way by most of the departments in the school. These groups furnish programs for the school, for the Parents' Association, and for Board of Education functions.

The course in music includes three or four years of theory and composition, a year of music survey, instrument training with correlative assignment to orchestra or band, or voice training with appropriate assignment to choral groups. The training in voice and instrument offers

a wide variety of experiences in singing and playing, all articulated
with the study of theory, music analysis, and music survey. Voice
students are assisted by the department of languages through the
medium of "Languages for Voice" courses, in which instruction is given
in German, French, and Italian. In the third year, qualified students
may elect such additional courses as piano accompanying, advanced
composition, dance band and arranging, and conducting.

The course in art includes three or four years of studio practice
with instruction in crafts and a year of art survey. The first year
is exploratory, giving the student an opportunity for creative expression with a variety of media. The second year is devoted to a study
of drawing, color, and composition in special media such as oil and
watercolor. The third year provides opportunity for specialization.
The student may choose architecture, painting, graphic arts, advertising
arts, or sculpture. He may elect costume design, textiles, stage
design, or ceramics.

The community resources of a great center of population are used
in various ways by the school. Music survey classes attend rehearsals
and performances in concert halls and opera houses. Art students work
on problems that require visits to museums, factories, department
stores, and architectural centers for research. Professional artists
and musicians have generously volunteered to come to the school to
lecture to certain groups or to give demonstrations. On occasion,
foremost composers have been commissioned to write musical compositions
especially for the school's needs.

*   *   *

STUYVESANT HIGH SCHOOL, NEW YORK 3, NEW YORK
Leonard J. Fliedner, Principal

*

Stuyvesant High School is a special four-year science school for
boys in the New York City school system. It has an enrolment of about
2,800 and a staff of about 110 teachers. Its purpose is to provide a
high-quality academic course for selected pupils, with emphasis on
science, mathematics, and mechanic arts. Opportunity is also provided
for specially qualified boys to take advanced courses in mathematics
and science, some of which lead to advanced standing in college.

Students are recruited from all sections of the city by sending
members of the Stuyvesant honor society to address groups of pupils in
the lower schools. Students who wish to enter file applications and
are given entrance examinations in mathematics and English. The results
of these tests, plus consideration of previous record, I.Q., and personality, determine entrance. Each year about 2,500 applications are
received for the 800 places in the entering class. The average I.Q. for
the student body is 130.

One curriculum is offered to all students, consisting of English,
social studies, language, science, mathematics, mechanic arts, fine
arts, music, and health education. Many elective choices are available

in advanced mathematics and science. A few special scholarship classes
are offered to students with previous high achievement. Nearly all the
courses are organized for school-wide regular classes. Some use is
made of homogeneous groups, and there is some provision for acceleration. All courses are presented with a view to stimulating a select
student body.

The work of the mathematics department is a good example of the
Stuyvesant program. Every course offers material beyond the normal requirements of city and state syllabi. For example, use of the quadratic
formula is part of the ninth-year course, and content from applied
mathematics is added. Assembly programs are frequently given over to
the mathematics department. In some classes students are asked to do
research and make historical or biographical reports pertinent to their
studies. A mathematics society meets every week. Students, teachers,
and outside speakers lecture on topics of interest to the members. A
teacher-coached mathematics team competes in contests with about fifteen
other teams of the city. The Mathematics Survey is published annually
by the students.

There are honors classes, beginning with tenth-year mathematics,
in which special treatment is given the subject by select teachers. At
the beginning of the first term of the eleventh year, certain students
enter a special class which completes eleventh-year mathematics and
takes advanced algebra and solid geometry, all in a year. This course
also includes many advanced topics, such as spherical trigonometry and
determinants, and allows students to take the extra elective. In the
twelfth grade, two college-level elective courses are offered: survey-
ing and calculus. Both have been recognized for advanced credit in
certain colleges.

Another example of the Stuyvesant program is the activity of the
physics department. Classes in experimentation and research are open
to boys who have completed one year of physics and who demonstrate
sufficient ability in physics, mathematics, and mechanics. They study
a number of classical topics, learn basic research procedure, pursue
original investigations, and make reports on their work. Physics I
honors-class members are selected on the basis of their work in chemistry,
English, and mathematics. Further selection precedes enrolment in the
Physics II honors class. These are college-type courses dealing with
modern theory, derivations, and technological applications.

Field trips to museums and laboratories and participation in
science fairs and the Westinghouse Science Talent Search are also a part
of the Stuyvesant program.

* * *

* * *

THE CLEVELAND PUBLIC SCHOOLS, CLEVELAND, OHIO

Dorothy E. Norris, Supervisor of Major Work Classes

*

The Cleveland public schools serve a cosmopolitan city of about 1,000,000 people. The program for the gifted in these schools provides for homogeneous groupings called "Major Work Classes." There are 38 of these classes in 22 of the 119 elementary schools of the system, offering an enriched program of studies. Each of these classes is housed in a regular school building and is an integral part of that school program. That is, although the gifted students have most of their subjects in their special classes, they take physical education, music, and crafts along with the rest of their age group and participate in all other regular school activities. In addition to the elementary Major Work Classes, there are three in the junior high schools and three in the high schools. Altogether, about 1,500 of the total enrolment of some 115,000 in the public schools are served in these special classes.

Since the elementary-school program is the most extensive, it is singled out for description in this summary. Any child measuring 125 I.Q. or over on a Binet test is eligible for a Major Work Class, if his maturity, social adaptability, emotional stability, and health are satisfactory. Candidates may be recommended for individual testing by teachers or staff members on the basis of classroom performance or group intelligence- and achievement-test results. Parents must give consent for the child to enter the program and must accept responsibility for getting him to one of the schools where the special classes are offered.

Any school may set up a Major Work Class, provided that it has a nucleus of gifted children and is within reach of public transportation so that students may come in from other school areas.

Groups consist of about 25 students. Usually Grades I, II, and III are housed in one room, as are Grades IV, V, and VI. The curriculum for these classes includes reading, spelling, arithmetic, language, art, music, science, safety, health, physical education, home economics, industrial arts, foreign languages, social studies, and instrumental music. Classes are informally arranged, and a permissive atmosphere is maintained. Because of their ability to learn more quickly, these students branch out on a program of work suitable to their ages and interests but not encroaching upon the work of grades beyond. Such enrichment is brought about by opportunities provided for certain activities and experiences and by the methods of instruction. Among these opportunities are special instruction in art, intensive work in language and literature, typewriting, writing and producing plays, making reports to the class, reviewing books, and writing articles for school newspapers.

French is also studied. Beginning as early as the primary grades, these children, through games, songs, and dramatizations, secure a foundation for the later study of French and other foreign languages.

Presenting the five-minute daily talks, making reports in geography and history, and presiding as leader in the literature groups provide opportunities for learning to speak effectively and well.

Students are encouraged to branch out in their reading into books of science, history, biography, travel, informational fiction, and poetry. They are kept in touch with the best in children's books through the literature-study group and by contact with the Junior Literary Guild.

Emphasis is given in classwork to national and world affairs, in an effort to increase understanding of social obligations and awareness of the world at large.

No one method of class instruction is used exclusively, but a socialized procedure is favored, with the teacher as an interested participant of the group. The work is planned in large units, a suitable method for these children because of their long interest span. It has been found that social studies, lieterature, and group projects lend themselves well to this procedure. Usually arithmetic, in which pupils progress at varying rates of speed, is on an individual basis. Some drill is used. Tests of various kinds are frequently employed to measure progress. Independent study is required, and help is not given until it is needed.

Besides participating in group activities, each pupil has the experience of carrying on a piece of work (resembling research) along some line of his own interest. This is finally presented to the class and is discussed and evaluated by the group.

Opportunities for learning by observation and direct experience are provided by trips to museums, the symphony hall, the zoo, parks, stores, mills, industry, and the docks.

The school is active in parent education. A group meets once a month to discuss gifted children. School psychologists are available to counsel the children when necessary, and teachers and supervisors work closely with parents. The parents' group also helps with the extracurricular activities of the program and promotes publicity in the community.

* * *

THE UNIVERSITY SCHOOL, OHIO STATE UNIVERSITY, COLUMBUS 10, OHIO

Paul R. Klohr, Director

*

The University School, an experimental laboratory school, is located on the campus of the Ohio State University, where it serves in the teacher-training program of the College of Education. Total enrolment in the lower school (kindergarten through the sixth grade) and the upper school (Grades VIII through XII) is about 450. There is a staff of 35 teachers. The University School operates no special program for gifted students, but, by reason of its nature and the resources at its disposal, a program of high caliber is offered to all students.

The school staff perceives giftedness in a child to mean more than the most effective measure of his mental ability. It also involves, in their judgment, special talents in such fields as art, music, the dance, and physical activities. Accordingly, although major emphasis is placed on general education for all children regardless of special interests, a second component of the curriculum is the number of special fields into which individual children are guided because of their interest and abilities. These groups tend to be homogeneous in terms of these criteria.

There is much individualization of instruction within both the general education and the special-interest areas. For example, basic texts are rarely used as instructional materials for groups. Rather, the library serves as a major resource, with reading material commonly ranging in a seventh-grade class, for example, from fifth-grade reading level to the adult level.

Acceleration for a student from one grade level to a higher one is based on total staff judgment. In general, the principle of keeping a child with his own age group and accomplishing acceleration through greatly enriched learning experiences characterizes the outlook of the staff.

The activities on the elementary level have been developed on a problem-solving basis. The work for any given period of time in each grade is organized around a central theme or problem which is of value in terms of the growth and development of the children and is of interest to the group. This large central problem is selected co-operatively by the teacher and the pupils and is subject to the approval of the entire staff. All the exploration collection of information, firsthand and vicarious experiences, expression, organization, and evaluation that are necessary for an understanding of this large problem comprise what is called a "Group Study" or "Unit of Work." A Group Study continues as long as there are major problems to solve or areas to explore, which may mean a few weeks or an entire year. However, except for seasonal studies, those planned in the elementary grades usually continue for the school year. The main thread of the Group Study is not essentially social studies or science. It is a composite of many areas of learning and experience. Any area which offers assistance in solving the problem is utilized.

The secondary-school curriculum provides for the general education of the students through the core program and offers opportunities in terms of special interest through the electives program. The core program consists of common learnings required of all students and provides experiences that cut across conventional subject-matter lines. These experiences are selected so as to include those that are in harmony with adolescent needs and interests and will help them meet adequately the problems of living in a democratic society. The core program makes up approximately half of the school day in Grades VII, VIII, and IX, and approximately one-third of the day in Grades X, XI, and XII.

* * *

* * *

DAYTON BOYS' CHOIR, DAYTON ROTARY CLUB, DAYTON, OHIO
S. Norman Park, Director

*

The Dayton Boys' Choir is a musical group sponsored by the Rotary
Club of Dayton, a manufacturing and commercial center of about 400,000
people. The choir is directed by one of the club members who is also
supervisor of music in the public schools. About 90 boys of from nine
to eighteen years of age are enrolled each year, from all parts of the
city and vicinity. The purpose of the group is to present an opportunity for boys to develop musically, socially, and personally. Rehearsals are held in a city church, twice a week in the evenings.
Concerts are presented in various cities of Ohio and neighboring states.

Boys are referred to the director by teachers and parents or apply
for admission to the choir on their own initiative. Voice and music-
reading tests are given twice a year, and the best are added to the
group as voices are needed. A long waiting list exists.

In the rehearsals and concerts the development of leadership and
good social relationships are stressed, as well as learning about music
and singing. The director is assisted by the student officers, particularly by the president, who leads the group upon occasions. Gifted
members of the choir do solo-work, and encouragement is sometimes given
to boys to take private voice or piano lessons or to go on with music
after high school.

Rehearsals are held twice a week for two hours at a time. Prompt-
ness and perfect attendance are required. The first ten minutes of
each meeting are devoted to musical exercises, the rest of the time to
learning the concert numbers. Some of the members of the choir can
read music, others learn by rote. All music is memorized, as nothing
is held in the hands during concerts. The choir sings various types
of selections, both sacred and secular, including many of the Waring
choral numbers. Programs are presented to private clubs, civic groups,
churches, public assemblies, and various conventions.

* * *

MALVERN SCHOOL, MALVERN AND FALMOUTH ROADS, SHAKER HEIGHTS, OHIO
Florence E. Gabriel, Principal

*

Malvern is an elementary school, one of the public schools of
Shaker Heights, a suburb of Cleveland, Ohio. The school community is
a privileged one, made up of people in the professions and in executive
positions in industry. Though few of the residents are of great wealth,
the neighborhood is one of residents able to avail themselves of

opportunities above the average. The enrolment of the school is about 425, in seventeen class groups in the kindergarten and the six grades. Classes are heterogeneous, each group made up of the usual range of higher- and lower-ability students. As the gifted evidence themselves in each regular art, music, English, science, and social studies classroom, they are offered enriched experiences designed to stimulate their giftedness and develop leadership ability.

Intelligence- and achievement-test results, school records, and observation by teachers serve to identify the gifted. The actual number of children identified at any one time as gifted is about 120, or more than a quarter of the total enrolment. Eleven teachers have special responsibilities for these children.

In English class these students write business letters or letters of acknowledgement or sympathy, as occasion demands. They write compositions not required by class assignment, head reading committees, or make speeches in class on behalf of Red Cross and community fund drives.

In science class the gifted students help keep the group informed about current science, participate in the formation of committees for study, and assist in the preparations for science trips. Simple experiments are performed, and a well-equipped library provides science newsletters and magazines for supplementary reading. A science club meets once a week.

In the social studies, gifted students make more extensive reports on topics being studied by the group. Often this includes the making of maps and charts, writing biographies, or keeping the class up-to-date on current events. They may also help other pupils with their work.

Specialized teachers in music and art provide for the gifted in these areas.

Opportunities that Cleveland provides for field trips are also a part of the enrichment program. School buses and helpful mothers take groups to libraries, the Art Museum, the Historical Museum, the Natural History Museum, freighters on Lake Erie, the Baldwin Reservoir, food terminals, bakeries, dairies, factories, stores, and galleries.

* * *

THE PORTLAND PUBLIC SCHOOLS, PORTLAND 8, OREGON

Clifford W. Williams, Administrative Director,
Gifted Child Project

*

The program for gifted children in the Portland, Oregon, public schools features a comprehensive plan for the identification and development of creative, intellectual, artistic, and leadership capacities. In the 14 elementary schools presently active in the program, this is accomplished by enrichment in the regular class program and through the formation of special classes. In the 5 high schools now participating, enrichment in the regular classroom, special sections of regular classes, and elective seminars are employed to carry out the program.

The project's most extensive plan for identification is centered in the fifth grade. Approximately one-third of the fifth-grade children are recommended for further testing in connection with the project, on the basis of teacher judgment, the California Test of Mental Maturity, and achievement-test scores. The Thurstone Primary Mental Abilities test is then administered, and children scoring consistently high or those having exceptionally high scores on one or more tests are checked for further study, with a view to enrichment of their school programs.

Children are also screened for exceptional talent in the areas of art, music, mechanical comprehension, creative writing, creative dance, creative drama, and social leadership. Methods of talent identification combining standard tests with other techniques developed by school committees have been devised for these purposes.

A distinguishing feature of the Portland program, and the one which probably has contributed most to its success, is the practice of designating a teacher in each building to act as co-ordinator for the program. Each co-ordinator is released from sufficient teaching duties so that half of each day can be spent in scheduling consultants, programing and counseling students, ordering books and materials, and keeping records. The importance of the co-ordinator, with specific duties and time to work, cannot be overestimated.

The type of program for able students in each of the participating schools varies, depending on the community of the school, the school and its faculty, and the children being served. Classroom procedures within a school also vary, but emphasis is placed on a variety of materials and practices, independent exploration, critical thinking, and attention to leadership capabilities. Although it is not the policy to group gifted pupils separately, some small special-interest groups meet for short periods two to five times a week for special studies in such areas as mathematics, foreign languages, science, creative writing, rhythms, music, creative drama, and social leadership.

As students leave the elementary schools, eighth-grade teachers and principals make recommendations to the high schools concerning students whom they feel to be intellectually gifted or to possess special talent in art, music, athletics, or social leadership. These recommendations are based on intelligence- and achievement-test scores and other knowledge of student ability and personality. In high school the Ohio State University Psychological Test is given to approximately one-third of the ninth-grade class, selected on the basis of seventh-grade intelligence-test scores and elementary-school and ninth-grade teachers' recommendations. The upper third of these, constituting about 11 or 12 per cent of the ninth-grade class, plus those students designated as possessing special talents, are given the additional attention provided by the project for the gifted in the high schools.

In the ninth grade this program usually takes the form of grouping and special project assignments in the regular classroom. Three high schools are engaged in an extensive experiment to determine the effect of selective classes on students, teachers, and methods. These classes offer more advanced reading and investigation; provide an opportunity to develop organizing, analyzing, and generalizing abilities; offer chance for the development of various forms of creativity; seek to utilize and encourage individual talents; and stress leadership and group membership training. A detailed report on this experiment will be published in September, 1955. In the tenth grade, seminar-type classes have been organized. Usually these classes take the place of a study hall for the participating students and involve activities in some selected regular subject.

In the eleventh and twelfth grades, selected students are invited to join in a program of individual and group study. These special groups deal with social science, literature, science, or mathematics and generally take the form of seminars attended by the students, high-school faculty members, and visiting professors from near-by Reed College. The seminars may serve to accelerate achievement in a special field, so that college can be entered at an advanced level, or to broaden interests and develop intellectual qualities which will serve as a foundation for later educational experience. Student initiative and active participation are stimulated by reducing the size of the classes and by encouraging informality. Discussion is based on common reading or arises from individual study and reports.

A particular feature of the Portland project is the close collaboration with Reed College. Representatives of this and other institutions of higher learning have participated in the planning of the project, conducted workshops, contributed to the high-school seminars, and assisted in testing and evaluation.

The Portland project also co-operates with the Quincy (Illinois) Youth Development Program, exchanging ideas on problems of research and program development.

Other important aspects of the program are its relation to parents and to the community at large. Project staff members are usually called on for several talks each week to various parent-groups, discussing the school enrichment program and the role of the home in the guidance of gifted children. When a special-interest class is planned in a school, conferences are held with the parents of the children involved.

Information concerning the work of the project is made available to the city at large by means of newspapers, radio, and television. Several radio and television stations have made it possible for students to appear in discussion and to perform in musical programs. Members of the staff appear before civic and community groups, describing the purpose of the project and emphasizing the role of the community in the development of its gifted children. Among the efforts being made by the community to encourage boys and girls with special abilities are those of the art museum and the library, which have been particularly interested and co-operative in making it possible for students to receive specialized training.

* * *

* * *

ALLENTOWN SCHOOL DISTRICT, ALLENTOWN, PENNSYLVANIA
Ethel M. McCormick, Assistant to the Superintendent

*

The Allentown elementary schools are a system of 21 schools with a combined enrolment of about 15,000, in an industrial and commercial city located approximately 50 miles from Philadelphia. Allentown has a population of about 110,000 and serves as a trade center for the Lehigh Valley. The program for the gifted in these schools draws chosen students from each school of the district to a special group of three classes, approximating Grades IV, V, and VI, which occupy one wing of a school. In these classes about 84 students and their 3 teachers participate in an enriched learning program.

A group intelligence test is used as the first screening device, during the second semester of the third year. All children having an I.Q. of 120 or more are given a standardized reading test. Those making a score of fifth grade or better are then given the Wechsler Intelligence Scale for Children. A pupil must make a full-scale score of 125 or more in order to be invited to join the special group. Parents' consent is also required.

The program is divided into two parts: basic skills introduced at each grade level and special-interest programs to suit the particular class. In addition, conversational Spanish is taught at all three levels, as well as typing in the sixth grade. Special teachers are available for reading, art, music, and physical education.

One of the enrichment projects is a book-reading and reviewing activity. The school subscribes to several publications that carry reviews of children's books (Elementary English, University of Chicago Book Center, Junior Libraries, and the New York Times). The children read a number of reviews, compare them, and decide what books should be ordered. These are read and discussed, and the reviews are evaluated. They then write their own reviews, the best of which are sometimes published in the local press. Decisions are formed as to what grade and interest level the books will appeal to, and recommendations are made as to which the school libraries should purchase.

The Spanish classes feature conversation, games, and original songs, poems, and plays.

In the typing class the children learn the keyboard and other parts of the typewriter and their uses. Routine exercises for skill and speed are followed by the typing of class and school activity materials.

Use of community resources is made as interest designates. For example, when a study was made of the county in which Allentown is located, exhibits of raw and manufactured products were assembled, and representatives from industry were invited to speak to the class.

* * *

* * *

GEORGE SCHOOL, BUCKS COUNTY, PENNSYLVANIA
Richard H. McFeely, Principal

*

George School is a Friends' boarding school for boys and girls
in Grades IX through XII. It is located in a country setting in
eastern Pennsylvania, 25 miles northeast of Philadelphia. About
450 students are enrolled, all of whom are in the four years before
college entrance, and there are 39 full-time faculty members. This
school operates a sequence plan of education. Most of the students
enter school in the first or second class. At the beginning of the
second class, students of similar aptitudes and interest form a
division, which for three years follows a curriculum particularly
planned for it. In turn, each division has three sections. Most of
the specially gifted of the school are enrolled in the top section of
one of the languages, natural sciences, or American relations divisions
and receive enriched courses. A few gifted are in the first-year,
exploratory division. Special opportunities are also provided for
those gifted in fine arts, woodwork, music, or other forms of expression.
The school is working on the College Admission with Advanced Standing
Program and selects the most able from the three divisions for special
English and mathematics classes. Individual acceleration is also
provided for in certain classes. In all, about 20 teachers and 150
students are involved in special activities for those of superior
ability.

In the ninth grade, students are placed in one of the five
sections of the exploratory division on the basis of ability, past
performance, and experience. Before the beginning of the second year,
each student is entered in one of the three sections of the three
divisions, so that the groups are as homogeneous as possible. Judgment
is made on the basis of scores on the American Council on Education
Psychological and the Diagnostic Reading tests, interests as revealed
by the Kuder Preference Record, student's choice of division, student's
performance, teachers' estimates, and anecdotal evidence. In general,
two kinds of giftedness are recognized: general intellectual giftedness and giftedness. in special fields, such as in music, art, dramatics,
or shop.

Each group of students has an adviser, who starts with the group
in the tenth grade and continues with them until they graduate. This
adviser plans the educational program with the teachers of a gifted
group.

Classes in English, fine arts, shop, science, mathematics, languages, social studies, and religion offer enrichment, and in some
cases acceleration, for gifted students.

For example, in the foreign-language division the possibility of
taking six to ten years of language study is presented, combining
Latin and French, French and German, Latin and German; or Latin,
French, and Spanish. On the basis of three or four years of French and

German, students are admitted to literature courses in college. Students also participate in the National French Contest. Language tables in the dining-room and an orientation discussion group on Saturday nights prepare students for going to France and Germany to participate in the Experiment in International Living and work camps. Affiliated schools in Germany exchange students with George, and college admission with advanced standing is offered these exchange or work-camp students. The program in the language classes is flexible, and its level depends on class ability and interest. French, German, and Spanish films are frequently used; and plays, songs, and games are featured in the annual French and German events at the school.

As another example of enrichment and acceleration at George, a superior student in mathematics may take a departmental examination to receive credit for a course without any classroom instruction in the subject. Or a student may detach himself from a class and progress at his own rate. Special classes in analytic geometry or calculus prepare students for college admission with advanced standing. Small numbers permit individual instruction in class and frequent consultation periods. Numerous references are used in classroom work, and outside reading is encouraged.

* * *

PITTSBURGH PUBLIC SCHOOLS, PITTSBURGH 13, PENNSYLVANIA

Earl A. Dimmick, Superintendent of Schools

*

The Pittsburgh public schools are a system of kindergartens, elementary, junior high, senior high, vocational, and special schools serving 79,000 students in this city of 679,000 people. The program for the gifted in these schools involves about 1 per cent of the pupils and covers the whole school system. Its purpose is to provide opportunities for children of unusual talents and abilities to grow in a way that will match their gifts. The major means used to accomplish this purpose is enrichment. Some special features are a scholarship program for outstanding pupils, art classes, science (nature-study) activities, and a school science fair, all maintained in co-operation with community organizations. In the elementary schools the program includes the subject areas of arithmetic, language arts, science, social studies, art, library, music, and health and physical education. In the secondary schools it includes mathematics, science, foreign languages, journalism, and speech.

For purposes of identification, the gifted elementary-school child is defined as one with a Binet I.Q. of 130 or above and/or demonstrating consistently superior performance in any given field. In the secondary schools the gifted student is thought of as one whose mental capacity to do school work is far above that of the average child. Identification of the gifted is a continuing process shared by teachers, principals, and administration, from the earliest intelligence and achievement testing given in the elementary school until graduation from high school.

No elementary school in Pittsburgh is considered as a special center for gifted children. Each develops its own program to meet the needs of the students enrolled. Acceleration may be used after consideration of the physical and social adjustment factors. Gifted children are not placed in special classes, but there is separation to the extent that the gifted child is with the typical class for most of his activities and is taken from that group to have opportunity to do work on particular projects. There is also some use of partial grouping, as in the Colfax School. Under this arrangement the gifted spend half of each day in a workshop and the other half with their chronological age groups.

Through enrichment--the major procedure adopted to meet the needs of the gifted--a greater breadth and depth of experience are offered in the regular classroom for those capable of profiting from it. A manual has been published by the Pittsburgh schools to assist elementary teachers in providing this enrichment. Cumulative record cards supply teachers with information concerning intelligence and achievement-test results and grade expectancy, to aid them in the identification of the gifted and in checking their progress.

To supplement the enrichment activities of the elementary schools, a science field-trip program for exceptionally able sixth-grade students was recently inaugurated. Saturday visits include trips to the Planetarium, the Carnegie Institute, a steel mill, a construction corporation, a power plant, and a research laboratory. Another activity, soon to be effected, is the teaching of foreign languages in several elementary schools.

In the secondary schools the differentiated curriculum and the club activity program are the most general provisions for the gifted student. Recently a program was initiated to provide opportunity for qualified pupils (on the basis of I.Q., performance, and parents' consent) to transfer to one of three secondary schools established as centers for special study in languages, mathematics, and science. Other classes especially provided for gifted students are advanced chemistry in one school, English research in another, and speech and journalism classes in three others. Present plans call for the setting-up of foreign-language and algebra classes in several junior high schools and the giving of special emphasis to the academic curriculum in four high schools that have a high percentage of graduates going to college.

For many years the Buhl Foundation has supported the awarding of first-year college tuition scholarships to those high-school graduates of promising ability who are otherwise not financially able to enter college. This program is administered by the Allegheny County Joint Committee on Scholarship Aid, an organization composed of school and civic groups interested in high-school graduates of exceptional ability. This group receives recommendations from principals of the various schools of the system, administers mental, achievement, and other tests to those students recommended, investigates their economic and social background, and makes selections for the awards.

The Carnegie Institute conducts art classes on Saturdays and during the summers for those students of the Pittsburgh area who, in the opinion of teachers and supervisors in the public, private, and parochial schools, show marked ability in art. Initial registration is made in the fifth or eighth grade, and, depending on their ability to progress, young persons may continue this free training until they complete the tenth grade. Then they may be one of a closely screened group recommended for the high-school classes in the College of Fine Arts at the Carnegie Institute of Technology. In all, this specialized training may continue for eight years, until the students are ready for art school or college.

The Carnegie Institute also sponsors a yearly nature contest for elementary- and secondary-school children of the area. A nature-study list is made up each summer in preparation for the following year's contest. A sample list is distributed to those students interested. On this list are the names of a number of specimens to be identified, as well as questions to be answered in various fields of natural history. Those entering the contest for secondary-school students are also asked to write an essay. During the year, museum exhibits that contain nature-contest material are specially identified. Many students visit the museum during the year to view exhibits and talk with the curators. Some schools have formed special nature-study groups in connection with the contest. Each spring when the contests are held, prizes are given to individuals and schools scoring highest.

At the present time, the institute also conducts a nature club on Saturday for seventh-graders who, because of their interest in natural history and a flair for science, have been recommended for the club by a science teacher. Illustrated lectures and field trips feature the activities of this group.

In co-operation with the Pittsburgh Board of Public Education, the Buhl Planetarium sponsors a school-year program of science education. Under this program teachers bring their junior and senior high school classes to the planetarium, either for science tours or for demonstration-lectures that supplement classroom studies.

The school science fair is an annual exhibition held at the Buhl Planetarium and Institute of Popular Science for students in the Pittsburgh schools. Students bring to the fair scientific exhibits and demonstrations built by them in their workshops at home or school or in science clubs. Scientists judge the displays and award honors and prizes. The fair is sponsored by the Buhl Planetarium, the Pittsburgh Press, and the Associated Science Groups of Western Pennsylvania.

* * *

COLFAX SCHOOL, BEECHWOOD BOULEVARD, PITTSBURGH, PENNSYLVANIA

Hedwig O. Pregler, Principal

*

Colfax is a kindergarten and six-year public elementary school located in a community that is above average educationally and economically. It has an enrolment of over 1,000 children and a faculty of about 30 teachers. Its program for the gifted is an individual school project.

The purpose of the program is to enrich the curriculum without acceleration by grade, with emphasis on the development of mental skills. About 120 of the most gifted students are segregated for a part of each day into ability groups called "Workshops." The rest of the day is spent in the regular chronological age groups. All the teachers of the school participate in the program in some way.

The mentally superior child is defined as one measuring 130 or more on the Stanford Binet Test and showing advanced achievement.

In the primary grades all children spend the first half of the morning with their regular classes, at which time they have their social activities, sharing of experiences, music, games, safety, and character education and similar things normally done by an entire group. Midway through the morning, the children move into their skill subjects, at which time the mentally superior children leave for their Workshops.

In the upper grades the school is run on the platoon plan. The gifted children leave class when the group goes to the academic teacher and rejoin it for the special subjects like art, music, and physical education.

The purpose of the Workshop is to develop mentally gifted children in all aspects of their giftedness, individually and in a group of mental peers. Workshops are informally arranged. Each group is organized, and new leaders are frequently chosen so as to provide opportunity for leadership development and experience in co-operation. Discussions, research, reports, evaluation, sharing of ideas, pupil-teacher planning, and pupil-pupil planning are features of these groups.

The individual is given attention by some adjustment of work to his needs and interests and through special conferences with teachers. Emphasis is laid upon the acquisition of individual work skills and habits.

In addition to classroom experiences in the usual subject areas, to which typewriting and German are added, various field trips are made. Workshop children all have parent permission slips that allow them to leave the building on any excursion that may come up during the year. They visit the Carnegie Central Library every third week for books and research work and use the intervening weeks to visit any place that they may be interested in at that time. They see such places as the planetarium, museum, conservatory, weather bureau, courthouse, radio and television stations, firehouse, a newspaper, dairy, and fairs that come to department stores. They also visit the Nationality Rooms of the University of Pittsburgh, Stephen Foster Memorial, river locks, Gulf Refining Company open house, and the steel mills.

* * *

* * *

DALLAS PUBLIC LIBRARY, DALLAS, TEXAS

Siddie Joe Johnson, Children's Librarian

*

The children's librarian of the Dallas Public Library, on her own initiative but with the co-operation of her colleagues and the schools, conducts a creative-writing group for the interested and talented children of the city. Two classes of about 20 each, one of elementary- and one of high-school students, meet in the library once a week after school to read and discuss poems, essays, and stories.

At the beginning of each school year, notices announcing the meeting of the creative-writing group are sent out through the Board of Education to all school librarians, English, and Language-arts teachers. The leader of the group also talks to parents, teachers, and children, over the library desk, in clubs, in school auditoriums, and on her library radio program. The Dallas Council of Parents and Teachers assists further with publicity. Those students interested are invited to come to the meetings. Attendance is entirely voluntary.

The program is flexible. The leader usually reads some selected poetry written by a young person. Then the group reads poems, essays, or stories of their own. Discussion and criticism follow. Before the meeting is ended, time is spent in composition. Through these activities the leader tries to encourage the reading of good literature (particularly poetry) and observation of the world. Members become familiar with various verse and prose forms, and they are encouraged to write.

Before the group disbands at the beginning of each summer, an exhibit and some informal contests are held. Sometimes a brochure of the children's verses is mimeographed.

Some of the members' work has been published in newspapers and magazines. Participation in a state high-school poetry contest has consistently brought prizes, and several college scholarships have been awarded members of this group on the basis of their creative writing.

Visits are occasionally made to the history museum or to the library film department for a showing. Visiting authors are invited to speak, and once or twice the group has attended the afternoon session of the annual meeting of the Texas Institute of Letters.

* * *

* * *

PROGRAM FOR EARLY ADMISSION TO COLLEGE

John J. Scanlon, Fund for the Advancement of Education,
655 Madison Avenue, New York 21, New York

*

The Program for Early Admission to College is an experiment participated in by twelve colleges and universities, including Chicago,
Columbia, Fisk, Goucher, Lafayette, Louisville, Morehouse, Oberlin,
Shimer, Utah, Wisconsin, and Yale. Its purpose is to carry out and
study the effects of an approach to meeting the problem of articulation
of secondary and collegiate education. It involves admission to
college of students carefully selected for their academic ability and
personal maturity, who have not completed the last year or two of high
school but appear ready for college experience.

Each participating institution follows its own selection procedures, though usually appraising candidates more rigorously than
ordinary students. The major screening device used by all institutions
is a scholastic aptitude test. Achievement tests are also used to a
large extent, and considerable weight is given to the applicant's high-
school record in appraising academic promise. Final selection takes
various factors into account, though academic promise and personal
maturity are the most important. Most applicants who survive the
initial screening are interviewed personally by college officials or
alumni.

There is much variation among the twelve institutions in curriculum, teaching methods, freedom of student choice, and opportunity for
acceleration. The majority of the colleges give the accelerated
scholars the same academic treatment as any other entering Freshmen.
Accordingly, they typically take the prescribed courses in the social
sciences, natural sciences, mathematics, humanities, and often a
foreign language. Where the scholars are academically segregated, it
is usually to provide them with an enriched curriculum and higher
performance standards than the general student body.

As an integral part of the Program for Early Admission to College,
a follow-up study is being made of the scholars. They are being
compared not only with their classmates but also with specially selected
"comparison groups" made up of students of comparable aptitude who had
finished high school before entering college. A considerable body of
evidence has been and is continuing to be gathered relative to their
academic performance and social and emotional adjustment.

* * *

* * *

THE SCHOOL AND COLLEGE STUDY OF ADMISSION WITH ADVANCED STANDING

William H. Cornog, Executive Director, President, Central High
School, Philadelphia 41, Pennsylvania

*

The School and College Study is carried on by a committee representing twelve schools or school systems and twelve colleges. The purpose of the study is to assist strong secondary schools, both independent and public, in planning and teaching courses in eleven subjects conventionally taught to college Freshmen, in order that able students may proceed farther than at present in the standard studies of a liberal education. When in full operation, the advanced or honor courses in some of the subjects will start in the tenth and continue through the twelfth grade, preparing students for Sophomore-level work in these subjects at college.

A group of eighty-one scientists and scholars who were teaching in schools or colleges were organized into eleven subject-matter committees: English composition, literature, Latin, French, German, Spanish, history, mathematics, physics, biology, and chemistry. These committees defined and described standards for the first-year college work to be taught in the schools.

Seven pilot schools first introduced the advanced courses designed to meet the official standards. Other schools are now participating, and still others plan to present candidates for the advanced examinations. The twelve colleges of the study have agreed to consider for advanced credit, on the basis of examinations and other evidence of accomplishment, entering students who have studied in the experimental school courses or their equivalents.

A digest of the advanced courses and the examinations used as a basis for admission with advanced standing has been published in College Admission with Advanced Standing; Announcement and Bulletin of Information (January, 1954).

The procedure in each pilot school has varied. Students for the program are usually selected on the basis of past scholastic achievement, recommendation of previous instructors, aptitude, intelligence-test scores, anecdotal data of guidance officers, and parental approval. Faculty committees in each school usually assist the directors in organizing and developing the program. Special or honors classes in certain subjects already a part of the pilot school's program have in many cases been used as a basis for the college-type courses, rather than developing entirely new ones. Classes are usually smaller than average for each school.

* * *

* * *

THE SCHOOL AND COLLEGE STUDY OF GENERAL EDUCATION,
PHILLIPS ACADEMY, ANDOVER, MASSACHUSETTS
Alan R. Blackmer, Committee Chairman

*

The School and College Study of General Education is a co-operative effort by three eastern preparatory schools--Andover, Exeter, and
Lawrenceville--and three closely related universities--Harvard, Princeton, and Yale. Its general purpose is to integrate the work of the
school and college in the area of general education. In particular,
this study is an effort to plan and carry out the last two years of
secondary school and the first two years of college as a continuous
process, avoiding the waste often involved in the transition from
school to college, especially in the case of gifted students.

The program that this study aims to achieve and offers to students
is a general, liberal education with enough flexibility to meet individual needs, continuous motivation to learn, and provision through
enrichment and acceleration for them to learn at a rate commensurate
with their ability.

The program embraces all students in the last two years of the
schools and in the first two of the universities.

Four means of heightening motivation are advocated. Priority is
given to selecting and encouraging imaginative, creative teachers. The
schools offer more opportunity for independent work to their ablest
Seniors. Personal contact between university faculty and undergraduates
is facilitated through tutoring, seminars, conferences, and small classes.
Students are led to more active participation in their education through
the writing of papers and participation in discussion and problem-solving
activities.

The program of liberal education for the four years includes
fundamental English studies, foreign languages, mathematics, physical
and biological science, a social science sequence, literature, the
arts, and a course in values. These courses are planned to offer
knowledge and skills as well as experience in interpretation and generalization, and an effort is made to build sequences between and within
them so that no course stands in complete isolation. Flexibility in this
basic program allows patterning individual programs to emphasize particular interests. Some elective choices are permitted.

Two types of acceleration have been planned. One, progression in
strength, permits moving ahead at a pace commensurate with ability in a
particular area. This may be accomplished in the schools through major
field studies, research projects, and tutorial instruction. Admission
to advanced courses in college, on the basis of placement tests, is then
possible. The other type of acceleration opportunity is offered by an
experimental seven-year program, an alternative to the normal eight
years of high school and college. Students selected on the basis of
emotional stability, good social adjustment, and good health, as well
as intellectual qualifications, may enter college as Freshmen after the

year in school or as Sophomores after graduation from school.

* * *

HORACE MANN-LINCOLN INSTITUTE OF SCHOOL EXPERIMENTATION,
TEACHERS COLLEGE, COLUMBIA UNIVERSITY, NEW YORK 27, NEW YORK

A. Harry Passow, Director of Talented Youth Project

*

The Horace Mann-Lincoln Institute, an integral part of Teachers
College, was established to further American education through experimentation designed to improve school programs. The institute co-
operates with different types of public schools and colleges in
experimental attempts to solve curriculum, instructional, guidance, and
in-service education problems. Its staff, including members of several
departments of the college, spends a considerable amount of its time
working directly with school people in co-operating field laboratories.
Reports of this co-operative experimentation, as well as analyses of
fundamental educational problems and procedures, are published by the
institute and its associated public school personnel.

The Talented Youth Project, one of the institute's current undertakings, is designed to study various aspects of talent and to experiment
with possible modifications by which schools can improve their educational
provisions for the talented. The project is concerned with a wide
variety of talents--including the academic fields, the arts, mechanics,
and human relations--and the possible programs in various-sized schools
and communities.

The work of the project has three related aspects: (1) preparing
materials which summarize and interpret research on the talented and
their education; (2) providing assistance to schools in the stimulation
and development of their own experimental programs for the talented; and
(3) conducting basic studies in the nature and function of talent.

An exhaustive search of the literature has been made, and a number
of schools interested in developing better programs have been visited.
A pamphlet, Planning for Talented Youth: Consideration for Public
Schools, has been published to provide a framework within which schools
can consider the total problem of educating the talented as they begin
to develop their own programs for identifying and nurturing the talents
of their youngsters.

Co-operative studies are evolving with several school systems. In
one, an effort is being made to develop extensive identification procedures to see whether more talented youth can be uncovered. Research
into the achievement level of talented youth is under way to see what
factors affect the fruition of talents. Studies of the efficacy of
various administrative and instructional provisions at different grade
levels and for diverse subject areas are being explored with several
school systems.

Proposed is a study of attitudes toward talented youngsters by parents, teachers, other youngsters, and the talented youth themselves that might facilitate or block special school or community provisions for those with the capacity for exceptional achievement. Also of interest to the institute is the problem of how to marshal resources to provide for the talented without hampering provisions for others in the schools.

* * *

SCIENCE TALENT SEARCH AND NATIONAL SCIENCE FAIR, SCIENCE SERVICE
1719 N STREET, N.W., WASHINGTON 6, D. C.
Watson Davis, Director

*

Each year a Science Talent Search for the Westinghouse Science Scholarships is conducted by Science Service, an institution for the popularization of science with headquarters in Washington. This search is a broad-scale operation intended to stimulate interest in science on the part of secondary-school students. Its objectives are to discover and foster the education of boys and girls who give evidence of potential creative originality in science, to focus the attention of large numbers of scientifically gifted youth on the need for developing their scientific and research skill and knowledge, and to aid in making American adults aware of the varied and vital roles played by science.

Some 15,000 entry blanks and examinations are sent out to teachers and school officials each year, and about a fifth of them are returned as complete entries. Each student contestant is required to take the Science Aptitude Test, have school officials complete a personal data sheet and scholarship record, and write an essay of about 1,000 words on "My Scientific Project."

On the basis of the examination and the personal data-sheet information, the number of contestants is reduced to 300. From this number, 40 boys and girls are selected to be invited to the Science Talent Institute in Washington, D.C., to compete for the top scholarships. The remaining 260 contestants receive honorable mention.

In recent years, several state academies of science, by special arrangement with Science Clubs of America, have held state talent searches concurrently with the national competition. By entering the national Science Talent Search, students in co-operating states automatically enter their state science talent search and have a double opportunity to obtain scholarships or other recognition and assistance.

Another activity of Science Service is the Science Clubs of America. This organization aids some 15,000 science clubs in all parts of the world by encouraging experimentation in science. About a third of a million boys and girls are enabled, during six years of junior and senior high school, to do projects and conduct inquiries that acquaint them with the method and practice of scientific research.

Many of these clubs participate in the science fairs sponsored by newspapers and school systems in a number of cities. A National Science Fair, also sponsored by Science Service, culminates the activities of the local fairs. From local fairs the best exhibits of student projects are selected for entry into the annual National Science Fair. Not more than two finalists, usually one boy and one girl, are chosen from each community and sponsored to the National Science Fair by a local newspaper, college, or other organization. All finalists participate in a three-day program of scientific sightseeing and meetings with leading scientists as well as the public. Each finalist receives a medal, and those whose exhibits are judged the best share in the awards of scientific equipment and materials selected to help them in the furtherance of this study and experimentation.

BIBLIOGRAPHY

Bibliographies in the Field of the Education of the Gifted

A number of good bibliographies have been prepared in this field. Described below are a few that have been selected as particularly good by reason of their being up to date, comprehensive, annotated, or consisting of the most useful references.

Huff, William, and Perkins, M. Helen (comps.). "What Are we Doing for the Superior Child?" Northwestern University Reviewing Stand, Vol. XVIII, No. 15 (June 8, 1952). Consists of 21 references with brief annotations, highlighting the topics in this field.

Jewett, Arno (comp.). The Rapid Learner in American Schools: A Bibliography. Circular No. 395. Office of Education, U.S. Department of Health, Education and Welfare, May, 1954, Washington 25. Single copies available upon request. Consists of 114 references, without annotations, organized into two groups: (1) books and (2) pamphlets and articles. Covers a wide range of topics.

Loomis, Grace I. (comp.). A Survey of Literature and Research concerning the Education of the Gifted Child with Implications for School Practice. Curriculum Bulletin No. 97, Eugene, Oregon: School of Education, University of Oregon, 1951. Consists of 56 references, most of them briefly annotated, covering a wide range of topics.

Martens, Elise H. (comp.). In The Gifted Child, Chap. 15. Edited by Paul Witty. Boston: Heath & Co., 1951. Consists of 234 well-annotated references, organized according to the topics: "General or Over-all Considerations"; "Philosophy and Objectives"; "Physical, Mental, Emotional, and Social Traits"; "Organization of Local Projects"; "Curriculum Adjustments"; "Evaluation and Follow-up Studies".

Wilson, F. T. (comp.). The Gifted Child (No. 3 in a series of bibliographies). Washington 6: Issued jointly by the International Council for Exceptional Children and the Research Division of the National Education Association. Consists of 43 references, most of them briefly annotated, organized according to the topics: "Parent-Child Relations", "Classroom Procedures", "Medical Materials", "Psychological Research Studies", and "General References".

A Bibliography of Selected References

General: Covering a Wide Range of Topics

American Association for Gifted Children. The Gifted Child. Edited by Paul Witty. Boston: D. C. Heath & Co., 1951. p. 338.

A comprehensive compilation, nontechnical in approach, covering topics indicated by the chapter titles: "Progress in Educating the Gifted"; "Identifying Gifted Children"; "The Stanford Studies of the

Gifted"; "The Contributions of Leta Hollingworth"; "Some Observations of Highly Gifted Children"; "The Teacher of Gifted Children"; "Mental Hygiene of Gifted Children"; "Community Recognition of the Gifted"; "Nature and Extent of Educational Provisions for the Gifted Pupil"; "A High School of Science for Gifted Students"; "Search for Talent in Science"; "Experiences with Children Talented in the Arts"; "Administrative Problems in the Education of Gifted Children"; "Summary and Recommendations"; and "A Bibliography."

Educational Policies Commission. Education of the Gifted. Washington: Educational Policies Commission of the National Education Association and the American Association of School Administrators, in Education Digest, 1950. XVI, p. 88, (December, 1950), 1-3. Excerpts.

A report dealing with the education of gifted children on all levels: elementary, secondary, and higher. Shows the great social waste in the failure of gifted individuals to receive proper education. Emphasizes the need for educational opportunities for all, regardless of social or economic status. Makes recommendations for the consideration of both school and community. Holds that society is responsible for making adequate opportunities available.

Loomis, Grace I. A Survey of Literature and Research concerning the Education of the Gifted Child with Implications for School Practice. Curriculum Bulletin No. 97, Eugene, Oregon: School of Education, University of Oregon, 1951. pp. 34.

A bulletin discussing the characteristics of the intellectually superior child, reviewing the history of attitudes toward giftedness held by educators and others, outlining some practices in organization and procedure of programs for the gifted, and examining special programs which have been developed for children of exceptional ability in various city school systems.

The Gifted: What They Are Like; How They Can Be Identified

Bristow, William H., Craig, Marjorie L., Hallock, Grace T., and Laycock, S. R. "Identifying Gifted Children," in The Gifted Child, pp. 10-19. Edited by Paul Witty. Boston: D. C. Heath & Co., 1951.

A chapter dealing with the topics: "Concepts of Giftedness"; "Environmental Influences on the Gifted"; "Promotion of the Maximum Growth and Development of All Children"; "Factors Involved in Identifying the Gifted"; and "Further Research into the Problems of the Gifted."

Corey, S. M., and Others. "Discovery of Outstanding Talent in Youth," Teachers College Record, XLVIII (January, 1947), 260-68. Condensed in Education Digest, XII (April, 1947), 1-4.

A report stressing the need for the development of human resources as well as natural ones, the need for early identification of talent,

and the need for the identification of all kinds of talent. Suggests
some principles that should characterize any national identification
of youthful talent and makes some recommendations for action, involving the setting-up of a National Commission for the Identification of
Talent.

Havighurst, Robert J., and Others. "Types of Children Who Are To Be
    Helped: The Gifted," and "The Screening Program for the Study of
    Children," in A Community Youth Development Program, pp. 15-27,
    53-56. Youth Development Series, No. 1, Supplementary Educational
    Monographs, No. 75. Chicago: University of Chicago Press, 1952.

    Two chapters in a booklet describing the planning and initial
efforts of a community youth-development program. Discusses various
topics in the general area of describing and discovering gifted
children: children with abilities in special fields, children with
intellectual ability, children with creative ability; screening for
general intelligence, for special talent, for artistic talent, for
intellectual talent, for creative intelligence, for leadership, and
for athletic talent.

Strang, Ruth. "Mental Hygiene of Gifted Children," in The Gifted Child,
    pp. 131-62. Edited by Paul Witty. Boston: D. C. Heath & Co., 1951.

    A chapter discussing the mental health of gifted children and
young people: normal problems and perplexities of growing up, special
problems intensified by high intelligence, conditions that contribute
to maladjustment, and guidance procedures.

Terman, Lewis M. "The Discovery and Encouragement of Exceptional
    Talent," American Psychologist, IX (1954), 221-30.

    An article surveying studies of gifted children, describing their
typical characteristics, and discussing testing instruments that
facilitate their identification. Also briefly treats of educational
methods.

Understanding the Child, XVII (April, 1948), 33-64.

    An entire issue of this magazine is devoted to the problems of
understanding the gifted child. Prepared in collaboration with the
American Association for Gifted Children. Contains articles on
research, special problems, clinical studies, and other topics.
Includes an article by Rhea K. Boardman and Gertrude Hildreth on
"Adjustment Problems of the Gifted," and an article by Paul Witty on
"Thirty Years of Research on Gifted Children."

Zorbaugh, Harvey, Boardman, Rhea Kay, and Sheldon, Paul. "Some Obser-
    vations of Highly Gifted Children," in The Gifted Child, pp. 86-105.
    Edited by Paul Witty. Boston: D. C. Heath & Co., 1951.

A chapter reporting the work of New York University's Counseling Center for Gifted Children. Describes some examples of highly gifted children and offers some generalizations about the highly gifted, based on studies from the files of the Counseling Center and the work of Terman and Hollingworth.

The Gifted and Their Parents

Cutts, Norma E., and Moseley, Nicholas. Bright Children: A Guide for Parents. New York: G. P. Putnam's Sons, 1953. pp. 238.

A book designed to help parents bring up their children to make the most of their intelligence at home, in school and college, and in useful living. It deals primarily with children of I.Q. over 120, who are likely to profit most from education and, by virtue of their intellectual endowment, have the best chance of becoming leaders in later life.

Kent State University, Department of Special Education. Role of the Parent in the Education and Training of the Mentally Superior Child. Kent, Ohio: E. R. Oswalt, Kent State University, 1951.

A booklet prepared by parents and teachers for a conference on mentally superior children. Designed to help parents understand the emotional and social growth of the gifted child and more effectively participate in the full-time process of his education. Chapters are titled: "Emotional Adjustment," "Human Relations," "Health and Physical Education," "Art Activities," "Music," "Travel," "Hobbies," "Library," "Language and Creative Expression," "Science," "Guidance," and "The Parents and the Psychologist."

Teachers of the Gifted

Ryan, W. Carson, Strang, Ruth, and Witty, Paul. "The Teacher of Gifted Children," in The Gifted Child, pp. 106-30. Edited by Paul Witty. Boston: D. C. Heath & Co., 1951.

A chapter covering the topics: "The Kind of Teachers Gifted Children Want," "The Teacher in Action in Class," "Personal Contacts Outside of Class," "Preparation of Teachers of Gifted Children," and "In-Service Education of Teachers."

Selvi, A. M. "Preparing Teachers for the Education of the Gifted," Educational Administration and Supervision, XXXIX (December, 1953), 493-99.

An article discussing some of the problems involved in meeting the needs of the gifted, as well as those of the majority of the students, and examining some of the plans and policies proposed for solving these problems. Reviews a plan of education for preparing teachers of the gifted and suggests how these teachers might best be used in school situations.

Wilson, F. T. "Suggestions for the Preparation of Teachers of Gifted
  Children," Elementary School Journal, LII (November, 1951), 157-61.

    An article describing the courses that teachers of the gifted
should take and the skills and other qualities that should characterize these teachers. Generally reveals a neglected area in teacher
preparation.

Organization of Programs for the Gifted:
  Curriculum and Administration Problems

Atkinson, B. H. "School Administration and Gifted Students," California Journal of Secondary Education, XXIII (January, 1948), 54-56.

    An article outlining what the school administrator can do to
adjust his program so that it will also meet the needs of the superior
students.

Berry, Charles S. "The Gifted Child--a Future Leader," National
  Parent-Teacher Magazine, XXXVIII (March, 1944), 27-29.

    An article explaining the help which must be given to the more
gifted students if they are to realize their powers in adult life and
give society intelligent leadership.

Carlson, Edith Fox. "Problems in Educating the Highly Endowed," Journal
  of Exceptional Children, XIII (April, 1947), 201-4, 220.

    An article defending special classes for the gifted. Based on
experience with several special-class groups, over a period of six
years. Individual cases are cited in describing how special classes
can remove barriers to development.

Flesher, Marie A., and Pressey, S.L. "War-Time Accelerates, Ten Years
  After," Journal of Educational Psychology XLVI (April, 1955), 228-38.

    Compares 145 women who graduated from Ohio State University in
three years or less, during 1941-46, with a nonaccelerated group.
Concludes that the accelerates suffered little or not at all as to work
experience, health, academic work, social life, and postcollege
adjustment.

Hattery, Lowell H. "Why Waste Talent?" School and Society, LXXI
  (February 11, 1950), 81-84.

    An article maintaining that gross loss of talent occurs at every
stage of the educational process. Points out the major causes, including
(1) inferior instruction, (2) inadequate or no guidance, (3) absence of
individual remedial attention, (4) economic hardship, (5) uncorrected

physical deficiencies, and (6) lack of motivation. Urges systematic
identification and ways in which we can increase the motivation of
the able students. Points out the critical need of effective use of
talent in our society.

Justman, J. N., and Wrightstone, J. W. "Opinions of Junior High School
   Principals concerning the Organization of Special Classes for Gifted
   Children," Educational Administration and Supervision, XXXVII
   (November, 1951), 396-404.

   A paper presenting an analysis of the results obtained through the
administration of a questionnaire concerning the value of the special
progress classes (accelerated) to all junior high school principals in
New York City. Suggests greater flexibility in regulations, greater
opportunity for curricular enrichment, some changes in acceleration
practices, a comprehensive program of teacher education, and greater
attention to the problem of integration of the special progress class
with the remainder of the school community.

Kent State University. Conference on Mentally Superior Children.
   Bulletin, Vol. XXXVIII, No. 11 (November, 1950). pp. 31.

   A bulletin reporting a conference on the gifted. Deals with a
wide range of topics: identification, the keeping of records, planning
the curriculum, class organization, methods of guidance, adjusting to
special needs, and others. The emphasis is on what some schools are
now doing and what seems to be the best practice. Suggestions are
offered for teaching various subjects: language arts, social structures,
science, physical education, mathematics, art, music, dramatics, crafts,
commercial subjects, and others.

Oliver, A. I., Jr. "Administrative Problems in Educating the Gifted,"
   Nation's Schools, XLVIII (November, 1951), 44-46.

   An article outlining several methods used by school administrators
in providing for the gifted child, some devices which can be used by
teachers, the type of teachers needed, and how to meet the cost of such
a program. Maintains that enrichment is the crucial problem of education
for the gifted.

Philadelphia Suburban School Study Council. Guiding Your Gifted: A
   Handbook for Teachers, Administrators, and Parents. Philadelphia:
   Educational Service Bureau, School of Education, University of
   Pennsylvania, 1954. pp. 89.

   A booklet reporting the study of a number of problems. Includes
sections entitled: "Who Are Your Gifted?" "Why Be Concerned about Your
Gifted?" "How Can You Contribute to the Total Growth of Your Gifted?"
"What Organizational Practices Should You Consider?" "What Can You Do
through Groupings Especially Designed for Them?" "How Can You Organize
Your School To Study Your Gifted?" and others. Suggestions are offered
for teaching various subjects: social studies, mathematics, science,
English, foreign languages, and other fine arts.

Pregler, Hedwig O. "Adjustment through Partial Segregation: Bases for
  Effective Learning." National Elementary School Principal (Thirty-
  first Yearbook), XXXII (September, 1952), 241-46.

  An article describing the problems of educating the gifted and the
two basic methods most often depended on: acceleration or enrichment
of regular classroom work. Describes a plan of partial segregation used
successfully at the school of which she is principal.

Pressey, S. L. "Acceleration: Basic Principles and Recent Research," in
  Proceedings; 1954 Invitational Conference on Testing Problems,
  pp. 107-12. Princeton, New Jersey: Educational Testing Service, 1955.

  A report presenting the argument that able students should progress
more rapidly than the lockstep rate through school and college because
they develop more rapidly than the average young person and should get
into their productive careers earlier than occurs in the lockstep.
Points out a variety of ways in which the progress of superior youngsters
may be facilitated, other than by grade-skipping or lengthened school
year. Reports some research results indicating that wise methods of
acceleration expedite progress without hampering social adjustment.

Scheifele, Marian. The Gifted Child in the Regular Classroom. New
  York: Bureau of Publications, Teachers College, Columbia University,
  1953. pp. 84.

  A volume discussing a number of topics, involved in developing a
program for the gifted. Emphasizes the necessity for teachers, schools,
and communities to co-operate in the formation of policies and procedures. Enrichment is suggested as the type of program offering the
greatest opportunity for the achievement of goals, under existing
community circumstances.

Sullivan, John C. "Adequate Education for the Intellectually Superior
  Child," Journal of Exceptional Children, XIII (November, 1946),
  44-48.

  An article emphasizing the need for attention to the total growth
of intellectually superior children and for opportunities to develop
leadership in association with other children if they have the capacity
for leadership.

Weisskopf, E. A. "Some Comments concerning the Role of Education in
  the 'Creation of Creation,'" Journal of Educational Psychology,
  XLII (March, 1951), 185-89.

  An article discussing the problem of how educators can encourage
the development of creative abilities in students. Criticizes some
common educational practices and offers a few general suggestions.

The Community and the Gifted

Brumbaugh, Florence. "Gifted Pupils and Parents Use the Community as
    a Laboratory for Learning," National Elementary Principal, XXV
    (September, 1945), 29-32.

    An article describing ways in which parents, under the supervision
of teachers, assisted in carrying on both school and after-school
activities for pupils. The former included such things as the school
library, hobby clubs, Scouts, parties, and week-end affairs.

Havighurst, Robert J., and Others. Are the Community and School Failing
    the Unusual Child? University of Chicago Round Table, No. 735.
    Chicago: University of Chicago Press, 1952.

    The report of a radio panel discussion on the subject of what the
school and community can do for the gifted. Touches upon several topics:
what the gifted are like and how they can be identified, some types of
school provisions for the gifted, what one particular community is doing
for its gifted, and others. Appended to the discussion report is a more
detailed account of a community youth-development program now being
carried on.

Hobbs, Nicholas. "Community Recognition of the Gifted," in The Gifted
    Child, pp. 163-84. Edited by Paul Witty. Boston: D. C. Heath & Co.,
    1951.

    A chapter dealing with important factors in organizing community
programs, accounts of communities that recognize their gifted, community
co-operation in the interest of the gifted child, and national programs
under the heading of "Accounts of Communities," a number of programs in
dramatics, music, art, poetry, recreation, and crafts are described,
sponsored by schools, a museum, a library, a service club, and other
community organizations.

Lorge, I. "Social Gains in the Special Education of the Gifted,"
    School and Society, LXXIX (January 9, 1954), 4-7.

    An article reviewing the varying attitudes held by the community
toward the gifted and describing how programs for the gifted are now
demonstrating their worth. Outlines some of the most pressing needs
of society and maintains that there must be planning for the utilization
of one of democracy's basic resources: superior intelligence. Describes,
in general, the type of program that will accomplish this.

Sumption, M. R. "Let the Community Plan the Program for Educating Gifted
    Children," Exceptional Child, XX (October, 1953), 26-27.

    An article dealing with the need for more community participation in
planning the school program and how it might solve many of the difficulties
involved in operating a program for the gifted. Suggests several ways in
which a community can do its part.

Some School Programs for the Gifted

Board of Education of the City of New York. <u>Specialized High Schools</u>
   <u>in New York City</u>. Brooklyn 2: Board of Education of the City of
   New York, 1946. pp. 263.

     A volume describing the secondary schools in New York City
designed to provide special training for students with special needs
and interests. At least four of the sixteen schools center about
purposes which tend to select high-level-ability students: Brooklyn
Technical High School, High School of Music and Art, High School of
Science, and Stuyvesant High School.

Board of Education of the City of New York. <u>Gifted Children and Slow</u>
   <u>Learners in the Junior High Schools</u>. Brooklyn 2: Board of Education
   of the City of New York, 1953. pp. 34.

     Part of an annual report of the New York City superintendent of
schools. The section dealing with the gifted treats of special progress
classes, enrichment classes, special classes for the artistically
gifted, and classes for specialized forms of academic aptitudes.

P. F. Brandwein, <u>The Gifted Student as Future Scientist</u>. New York:
   Harcourt Brace & Co., 1955.

     This is a report by the chairman of the science department of the
Forest Hills High School describing the program which his department has
developed for the identification and development of students who are
gifted in science. On the basis of this program, he makes proposals
for local and national programs. He also has an interesting chapter on
the problem of selecting and training teachers for work with gifted
children.

Calgary School Board, Committee on Gifted Children. "Final Report on
   Practices in Other School Systems." Calgary, Alberta, Canada: Calgary
   School Board, February 10, 1954. pp. 9.

     A mimeographed bulletin reporting the results of a questionnaire
survey of some school systems, designed to find out to what extent and
with what success the three methods of dealing with gifted children
(enrichment, acceleration, and segregation) are being used. Includes
reports on schools in Allentown, Pennsylvania; Baltimore, Maryland;
Boston, Massachusetts; Chicago, Illinois; Cleveland, Ohio; Duluth,
Minnesota; Los Angeles, California; Milwaukee, Wisconsin; New York,
New York; Pasadena, California; and Portland, Oregon.

Hildreth, G. H., and Others. <u>Educating Gifted Children at Hunter College</u>
   <u>Elementary School</u>. New York: Harper & Bros., 1952. pp. 272.

     A book summarizing and evaluating ten years of work by Hunter
College Elementary School, an internationally known school for gifted
children. A comprehensive report, including such topics as: Organization

of the school, goals and curriculum, class organization, teaching methods, instructional resources, instruction in subject matter and academic skills, life in school, the school and community, parents as the school's co-workers, guidance and adjustment of gifted children, the preparation of teachers, and outcomes in achievement, skills, and attitudes.

Jewett, Arno, and Others. Teaching Rapid and Slow Learners in High Schools. United States Office of Education, Bulletin 1954, No. 5. Washington: Government Printing Office, 1954. pp. 97.

A bulletin reporting a survey of the status of adaptations for rapid and slow learners in junior, senior, and regular high schools enrolling more than 300 pupils. Summarizes questionnaire returns from about 900 schools, covering such topics as administrative provisions, techniques and methods used in discovering rapid-learning pupils, and instructional provisions in the several subject fields: English, social studies, mathematics, science, home economics, and industrial arts.

Loomis, Grace I. "Special Provision for the Gifted," in A Survey of Literature and Research concerning the Education of the Gifted Child with Implications for School Practice, pp. 10-23. Curriculum Bulletin No. 97. Eugene, Oregon: School of Education, 1951

A chapter describing some programs for the gifted in the following cities: Cleveland, Ohio; Los Angeles, California; New York, New York; Appleton, Wisconsin; Detroit, Michigan; Baltimore, Maryland; Birmingham, Alabama; and Brockton, Massachusetts.

Morrissy, E., and Others. "The Superior Child in the Baltimore Public Schools," Baltimore Bulletin of Education, XXXI (June, 1954).

A magazine issue entirely devoted to describing the Baltimore schools' program for the gifted. Reports general practices in identification, guidance, and instruction, as well as what some particular schools in the system are doing.

Pregler, H. O. "The Colfax Plan," Exceptional Children, XX (February, 1954), 198-201.

An article describing the arrangement for meeting the needs of the gifted at the Colfax Elementary School in Pittsburgh. Describes their special grouping plan. Mentally superior children are grouped together for a part of each day in a special workshop devoted to enriching each regular subject. The rest of the day is spent by the students in their own chronological age groups.

Some Special Projects Involving the Gifted

Integrating the Work of Secondary School and College

Coombs, Philip H. "Lessons from Recent Experiments in Articulation
   and Acceleration," in Current Issues in Higher Education, pp. 271-75.
   Washington: Association for Higher Education, National Education
   Association, 1954.

   An article reporting several programs of co-operation between
secondary schools and colleges that the Fund for the Advancement of
Education is supporting: the Andover, Exeter, Lawrenceville, Yale,
Harvard, Princeton project in the integration of the work of grades
XI-XIV; the Portland, Oregon, public schools-Reed College program of
enrichment; the Admission to College with Advanced Standing Program;
and the Program for Early Admission to College.

Jones, E. S., and Ortner, G. K. "Articulation of High School and
   College," Review of Educational Research, XXIV (October, 1954).

   An article reporting some studies of students who entered college
without graduating from high school and of high-school graduates who
entered college with advanced standing. Also describes the programs
that provide for these practices.

School and College Study of Admission with Advanced Standing. College
   Admission with Advanced Standing: Announcement and Bulletin of
   Information. Philadelphia: William H. Cornog, Executive Director,
   c/o Central High School, 1954.

   A bulletin describing an experimental program whose purpose is to
assist strong secondary schools, both independent and public, in planning and teaching courses in eleven subjects conventionally taught to
college Freshmen in order that able students may proceed further than
at present in the standard studies of a liberal education. Lists the
colleges and secondary schools participating in the program. Gives a
digest of courses and examinations used and outlines some of the procedures of the pilot secondary schools.

Search for Talent

Davis, Watson. "Search for Talent in Science," in The Gifted Child,
   pp. 235-42. Edited by Paul Witty. Boston: D. C. Heath & Co., 1951.

   A chapter describing an annual nation-wide search for science
talent among the Seniors of the secondary schools of the United States.

Some Organizations Interested in the Gifted

American Association for Gifted Children. 15 Gramercy Park, New York
   3, New York. Pauline Williamson, Executive Secretary.

An objective of this association is to "help find gifted children,
help them to use their abilities for their own satisfaction and the
benefit of others, and at the same time to maintain status with their
own groups." An article in Understanding the Child, XXII (1953),
121-24, describes this association and its work.

Horace Mann-Lincoln Institute of School Experimentation. Teachers
   College, Columbia University, New York 27, New York. A. Harry
   Passow, Director of Talented Youth Project.

This organization is an integral part of Teachers College and has
as its aim the furthering of American education through experimentation
designed to improve school programs. The Talented Youth Project, one
of its current undertakings, is studying various aspects of talent and
experimenting with possible modifications by which schools can improve
their educational provisions for the talented. A pamphlet, Planning
for Talented Youth: Considerations for Public Schools, has been
published.

International Council for Exceptional Children. 1201 Sixteenth Street,
   N.W., Washington 6, D.C. Harley Z. Wooden, Executive Secretary.

This council is a department of the National Education Association.
It is interested in handicapped and gifted children, their education
and welfare. The council publishes a magazine, Exceptional Children.